PERSPECTIVES ON THE HISTORY
OF ECONOMIC THOUGHT
VOLUME VI

THEMES IN KEYNESIAN CRITICISM AND
SUPPLEMENTARY MODERN TOPICS

Perspectives on the History of Economic Thought Volume VI

Themes in Keynesian Criticism and Supplementary Modern Topics

Selected Papers from the
History of Economics Conference
1989

Edited by
William J. Barber

Published for the History of Economics Society
by Edward Elgar

Published by
Edward Elgar Publishing Limited
Gower House
Croft Road
Aldershot
Hants GU11 3HR
England

Edward Elgar Publishing Company
Old Post Road
Brookfield
Vermont 05036
USA

British Library Cataloguing in Publication Data
History of Economics Society (Conference: 1989: Richmond, Va.)
    Themes in Keynesian criticism and supplementary modern topics:
    selected papers from the history of Economics
    Conference 1989. – (Perspectives on the history of
    economic thought, v. 6).
    1. Economics. Theories, history
    I. Title II. Barber, William J. (William Joseph) *1925–* III. Series
    330.1
Library of Congress Cataloguing-in-Publication Data
History of Economics Society. Conference (1989: University of
    Richmond)
        Themes in Keynesian criticism and supplementary modern topics:
    selected papers from the History of Economics Society Conference,
    1989 / edited by William J. Barber.
        p.   cm. – (Perspectives on the history of economic thought; v. 6)
        Conference held June 10–13, 1989 in Richmond, Virginia.
        Includes bibliographical references and indexes.
        1. Keynesian economics–Congresses.   I. Barber, William J.
    II. Title.   III Series.
        HB99.7.H57   1989
    330.15'6–dc20   90–14036
                                                                            CIP

ISBN 1 85278 364 8

Printed in Great Britain by
Billing & Sons Ltd, Worcester

Contents

PART IV SUPPLEMENTARY MODERN TOPICS

Introduction

William J. Barber

This volume and its companion – *Perspectives on the History of Economic Thought, Volume V: Themes in Pre-Classical, Classical and Marxian Economics* – are selected from more than 120 papers presented at the sixteenth annual meeting of the History of Economics Society which was convened at the University of Richmond in Richmond, Virginia, 10–13 June, 1989. Scholars from 21 countries participated in the discussions at this conference.

Most of the essays in Volume VI are concerned with some aspect of the thought and career of John Maynard Keynes. It is not surprising that this should be so. More than any other figure in the twentieth century, Keynes has set the agenda for economic debate. Economists of all analytical persuasions have been obliged to take note of his theories and to define their positions with reference to Keynes's work.

In the first paper, Rod O'Donnell explores dimensions of Keynes's intellectual posture which have frequently received less attention than they deserve. It is readily understandable why the bulk of the voluminous literature of Keynesian criticism has concentrated on Keynes as economist. Nevertheless, as O'Donnell argues, a thorough understanding of this multi-faceted thinker requires an appreciation of the philosophical traditions within which his thought was moulded. In particular, Keynes's positions on the role of the state in economic activity – which, at times, seemed to some observers to be less than consistent – cannot be adequately comprehended if detached from his political philosophy.

Robert W. Dimand provides an instructive analysis of Keynes's first writings in economics which were concerned with the monetary system of British India. This phase of Keynes's career has tended to be overshadowed by the achievements of his professional maturity. As Dimand demonstrates, the early studies of Indian currency and finance won recognition for their originality and for the author's willingness to challenge such orthodoxies as the gold standard. Moreover, they revealed a cast of mind about the international monetary order – one organized around a gold-exchange standard with fixed exchange rates – that was to re-emerge in the 1940s with Keynes's design for the Bretton Woods system.

The three essays in Part II address a common theme: the responses to the publication in 1919 of Keynes's *The Economic Consequences of the Peace*. This book, with its biting denunciation of the Treaty of Versailles, was a literary sensation and it established Keynes's reputation as a formidable polemicist. The contents were informed by his privileged vantage point as a member of the British Treasury delegation to the Paris Peace Conference – a post from which he resigned in protest. The nature of that protest, in turn, took highly visible form in *The Economic Consequences of the Peace*. Keynes regarded the handiwork of the negotiators in Paris as vindictive and immoral and he took particular aim at the settlements on German reparations (which he regarded as unjust and unworkable). This book vaulted Keynes into international prominence and the comment it attracted certainly contributed to nurturing a character trait that was to be persistent: that is, the author's sense of confidence that he could manipulate public opinion with his pen.

As J. A. Hemery shows, the actual impact of the book on British opinion in the immediate post-World War I years is not so easy to document unambiguously. Keynes clearly succeeded in 'setting the cat among the pigeons' and the analysis he offered won influential supporters. But there were others who questioned his 'patriotism', his discretion, and his tact in delicate matters of diplomacy. Hemery suggests, however, that the movement of British opinion towards revision of the Treaty was shaped more by concerns about the state of the domestic economy in 1921 than by Keynes's words. Even so, some of the 'economic consequences' for Britain that Keynes had forecast in the book seemed to be validated by events. And this, in turn, enhanced Keynes's credibility as an economic analyst.

Charles Blitch's essay inspects the reception of *The Economic Consequences of the Peace* in the United States. In America, as in Britain, the book was a best seller. American reactions, however, were dominated by Keynes's vitriolic portrait of President Wilson as a bumbling incompetent. This characterization produced some strain between Keynes and a number of the American economists who had participated in the negotiations in Paris. While the latter might have been sympathetic to Keynes's technical economic arguments, they resented the attack on Wilson, the liberal hero, and feared that it would feed the forces of reaction in American political life. Passages from *The Economic Consequences of the Peace* entered the Congressional Record in the Senate's debates over ratification of the Treaty of Versailles – which was defeated.

Keynes's book, as Domenico da Empoli reports, was also widely discussed in Italy. Indeed Keynes himself believed in 1920 that its contentions were accepted there almost universally. Much of the Italian readership, however, could identify with the attack on the negotiators in Paris primarily because they had frustrated Italy's aspirations for territorial gains on its Eastern frontier. The book's contentions on the economics of German reparations passed virtually unnoticed.

While the book was received quite differently in the three countries surveyed, its author achieved a notoriety in each which ensured that anything he might write later would not be ignored. It is to be hoped that the investigations presented in Part II will inspire others to undertake research along similar lines in Germany and France.

In Part III, two essays offer appraisals of Keynes's contributions from less than sympathetic perspectives. Gilles Dostaler examines the divergences – and some of the intersections – between the analytic programmes of Friedrich Hayek and Keynes. This essay brings to life the intellectual ferment of the early 1930s when two distinct strands of theorizing competed for supremacy: an Austrian-style analysis of capital theory that Hayek brought to the London School of Economics and a Cambridge-style of monetary theorizing that Keynes had extended and reformulated in the *Treatise on Money*. For a number of years in the middle 1930s, the outcome of that contest was uncertain. A Keynesian perspective appeared to have triumphed when the message of *The General Theory* was assimilated. But, as Dostaler indicates, the problems of the 1970s and 1980s have stimulated a fresh appreciation of Hayek's perspective. Instructive parallels can be drawn between the contours of the Keynes–Hayek debate in the 1930s and the latter-day controversies between 'neo-Keynesians' and 'new classicals'.

Leland Yeager's contribution provides a fresh perspective on the work of another critic of Keynesianism. Based for the greater part of his professional career in South Africa, William H. Hutt operated outside the mainstream of theoretical controversy in the 'years of high theory' sparked by the Great Depression. Hutt spoke with a distinctly individual voice, so individual, in fact, that his message was imperfectly understood. Like Hayek, he rejected the Keynesian emphasis on macroeconomic aggregates as determinants of economic performance. His analysis of unemployment focused instead on wage and price 'stickiness' that distorted market behaviour. Hutt's crankiness about labour unions – as well as his convoluted style of expression – put off at least part of his potential audience. Nevertheless, as Yeager notes, there are some striking affinities between Hutt's arguments and the later literature on the economics of market 'discoordination'.

The three essays in Part IV illustrate ways in which issues of long-standing can be enriched through modern reinterpretations. Hans Brems's contribution recreates the framework of Austrian time-interest analysis – originally set out by Böhm-Bawerk and subsequently extended by Wicksell – which concluded that a reduction in the rate of interest would tend to lengthen the period of production. He then investigates whether or not this finding would survive if the assumption of stationary technology (around which the original analysis was built) were to be relaxed. With technological progress incorporated into the model, Brems argues that a lower interest rate would encourage more frequent replacement of capital. This finding, set in a more dynamic context, reverses the result arrived at by those who pioneered in the development of this body of theory.

Bo Sandelin's contribution explores another aspect of capital theory in a re-interpretation of the 'Wicksell effect'. The problem addressed here turns on the revaluation of the capital stock associated with a change in capital that alters the interest rate and the wage rate. Modern approaches distinguish between a 'price effect' that alters the valuation of capital when technology is given, and a 'real effect' that induces a change in techniques as a consequence of variation in the rate of interest. Sandelin argues that Wicksell's 'complete model' incorporates both of these effects and that the claim that Wicksell failed to appreciate the 'real effect' is mistaken.

Charles M. A. Clark's chapter invites reflection on a question that is at once 'modern' and timeless: how applicable are the methods and models of the natural sciences to the social sciences? He traces the way economic and social theorists over the span of several centuries have sought to ground their models on orderly regularities linked with some conception of a 'state of nature'. The precise character of the appeal to a 'natural order' has shifted over time. After inspecting the levels of abstraction deployed in various traditions of theorizing, Clark suggests that the moral philosophers of the Enlightenment, the marginalists, and late twentieth century general equilibrium theorists have more methodological affinities than are commonly recognized.

Contributors

William J. Barber, Department of Economics, Wesleyan University, Middletown, Connecticut

Charles P. Blitch, College of Business and Public Administration, Old Dominion University, Norfolk, Virginia

Hans Brems, Department of Economics, University of Illinois, Champaign, Illinois

Charles M. A. Clark, Colleges of Business Administration, St. John's University, Jamaica, New York

Robert W. Dimand, Department of Economics, Brock University, St. Catharines, Ontario, Canada

Gilles Dostaler, University of Quebec in Montreal, Montreal, Canada

Domenico da Empoli, University of Rome 'La Sapienza', Rome, Italy

John Hemery, Institute for International Studies, University of Leeds, Leeds, England

Rod O'Donnell, School of Economic and Financial Studies, Macquarie University, Sydney, Australia

Bo Sandelin, University of Göteborg, Göteborg, Sweden

Leland B. Yeager, Department of Economics, Auburn University, Auburn, Alabama

PART I

INTERPRETATIONS OF KEYNES'S POLITICAL AND EARLY ECONOMIC WRITING

1 Keynes's political philosophy

Rod O'Donnell[1]

Introduction

Until recently, there have been no attempts at fundamental and systematic investigations of Keynes's political philosophy. Commentary there naturally has been, much of it instructive and scholarly, but three characteristics of the earlier literature stand out. First, it is miniscule compared to the vast output on his economics, despite the fact that his political writings are reasonably extensive.[2] Second, it has assumed that it is sufficient to rely on his political writings, supplemented where necessary by his economic writings.[3] And finally, it has failed to distil any fundamental philosophy of political thought capable of integrating all of Keynes's remarks into a consistent whole. Indeed, the implication of one of the most scholarly investigations of this type (Freeden, 1986, pp.154–73) is that Keynes's political position did not reflect any 'thought-out philosophical view'. The consequence has been that Keynes's political philosophy and political position have remained somewhat enigmatic, resistant to the probing of economists, political scientists and historians alike, and engendering a diversity of characterizations from conservative at one extreme to socialist at the other.[4] In the last few years, however, interest in Keynes's philosophical writings (published and unpublished) has grown, and new approaches to the problem have been taken by investigators such as Skidelsky (1983), O'Donnell (1982, 1989) and Helburn (1988).

This chapter has two objectives. The first is to demonstrate that the puzzle of Keynes's politics can be comprehensively resolved by means of a new approach. My claims here are that a definite political philosophy underpins Keynes's various political utterances, that this philosophy unifies remarks which *prima facie* seem disconnected, odd and even inconsistent, and that the key to the resolution is provided by Keynes's *philosophy of practical reason.*[5] It is *philosophy,* a source outside his political and economic writings, which provides the origin of Keynes's politics, and which gives access to the central chamber from which all pieces of the jigsaw can be viewed as a coherent whole. The traditional approach of taking his political and economic writings as adequate to the task leaves one endlessly wandering the corridors. Nevertheless these writings contribute one absolutely essential element, namely, his remarks on money. A related contention of the chapter is that Keynes's basic political framework, rather like his philosophical framework generally, underwent no radical changes during his adult lifetime. This is because the philosophical framework which germinated in 1903–4 and was further developed in the ensuing decade, provides the only framework within which all his subsequent political remarks can be given a consistent meaning. The first part of the paper outlines the essential features of this political philosophy.

The second object of the chapter is to locate Keynes's political position in relation to three major streams of political thought – conservatism, liberalism and socialism. It is argued that Keynes's overall position is a form of liberalism which has its centre of gravity to the left of centre, a feature which permits it, from a certain perspective, to be also regarded as a moderate form of socialism. The vital point is that Keynes's was a distinctive form of liberalism with its own philosophical foundations and its own agenda. It firmly rejected much of old liberalism, the classical *laissez-faire* position favoured by many of the founding fathers, but at the same time was not an offshoot of the New Liberalism of 1870–1914 which also rejected old liberalism. What is distinctive about Keynes's liberalism is first, that its tap-root was sunk deep in Moore's ethics, and second, that it gained additional nourishment from *parts* of Burke's writings. With this unique soil it is not surprising that the result was a distinct and unconventional variety of liberalism. A liberalism erected on Keynes's Moorean ethical foundations, moreover, entailed quite radical social transformations. Keynes himself once described his position as a form of 'liberal socialism'. But as regards socialism, it is impossible to understand Keynes's position until certain basic distinctions are made within the field of socialism, particularly as between Marxist and non-Marxist variants. The modern discussion of socialism, being preoccupied with Marxist versions, tends to overlook non-Marxist conceptions.

The puzzle
To illustrate the enigmatic nature of Keynes's politics, consider the clash seemingly generated by two passages taken from well-known articles in *Essays in Persuasion*. Written within only seven months of each other, each is in response to virtually the same question.

In 'Am I a Liberal?' of August 1925, Keynes asked whether he ought to join the Labour Party, and gave two reasons for saying no. The first focused on class. Labour was 'a class party, and the class is not my class', to which he added his famous remark that 'the *class* war will find me on the side of the educated *bourgeoisie*' (IX, 297, emphasis in original). The second reason centred on intelligence. 'I do not believe that the intellectual elements in the Labour Party will ever exercise adequate control ... and if ... control ... is seized by an autocratic inner ring, this control will be exercised in the interests of the extreme left wing' (IX, 297). This 1925 response creates the impression of a considerable distance between Keynes and left wing politics. It suggests that his ultimate sympathies were with the bourgeoisie and against socialist programmes of social transformation. The implication is of a political position in the centre, if not somewhat right of centre.

But in 'Liberalism and Labour' of February 1926, Keynes gave a quite different impression. The question posed is virtually identical – should the Liberal Party close down and swing over to the Labour Party? – and again Keynes resisted the proposal.

While most Liberals might be ready to support Labour from time to time, he argued they 'would not feel comfortable or sincere ... as full members of the Labour Party'. He then illustrated this remark with reference to himself.

> Take my own case. I am sure that I am *less* conservative in my inclinations than the average Labour voter; I fancy I have played in my mind with the possibilities of *greater social changes* than come within the present philosophies of, let us say, Mr Sidney Webb, Mr Thomas, or Mr Wheatley. *The republic of my imagination lies on the extreme left of celestial space* (IX, 308–9, emphases added).

This presents a radically different picture. Now Keynes is objecting to the Labour Party because it is *not left enough*, because its programmes of social change fall short of his own conceptions. His vision lay beyond the Fabian Socialism of Webb, beyond Thomas's trade unionism, and even beyond the revolutionary socialism advocated by Wheatley. The implication is now that Keynes takes his position to be considerably left of centre, further left even than certain factions of the far left.

This 'paradox' has gone unresolved and unremarked, largely as a consequence of the lack of deeper investigation of Keynes's politics. So far as the secondary literature is concerned, the former passage has gained the ascendancy, while the latter, proclaiming Keynes's self-perceived leftist tendencies, is often ignored. The former conforms to the conventional view that Keynes's politics were directed at saving capitalism from itself and making it work more humanely. The latter seems to be an aberration, a throw away line that can actually be discarded. This is a mistake, however, for within Keynes's framework the two passages are internally consistent and equally informative.

Keynes's political philosophy

Keynes's conception of politics
The dominant philosophical influence on Keynes was Moore's *Principia Ethica* of 1903, central to which was a firm distinction between means and ends. Within this means–ends framework, social sciences such as politics and economics occupied a particular position. They were means capable of contributing towards the ultimate ethical end of increasing the amount of intrinsic goodness in the world. More precisely, they were not *direct* means to goodness,

but means to the preconditions of goodness; that is, they could not themselves establish goodness, but they could create an environment conducive or necessary to the expansion of goodness. The notion of politics as a means to ethical ends emerged clearly in Keynes's early unpublished paper, 'Miscellanea Ethica', of 1905. This proposed a complete ethical treatise divided into speculative (or theoretical) ethics on the one side, and practical ethics on the other, within which latter was located 'the theory and methods of Politics'. Politics for Keynes was thus cast in a Moorean mould from the start – it was a subdivision of the theory of practical ethics or the philosophy of practical reason.

Two important conclusions followed. Firstly, political theory could not establish truths about ultimate ends, for only ethics could establish such truths. As the servant of ethics, politics could only provide truths about means. Consequently there were no ultimate political ends, no ideal forms of government, no political principles valid independent of circumstances, and no universally true abstract rights. 'Natural rights' were thus denied. The qualities such rights sought to protect might be good in an instrumental sense, but the rights could be legitimately infringed if they interfered with the attainment of greater intrinsic goodness. As it happens, however, significant degrees of individual freedom and security are preconditions of the pursuit of intrinsic goodness in Keynes's scheme, so that many of the most commonly advocated rights would be defended to a considerable extent. But in no sense are they inalienable or absolute, for they are not the ultimate end of political action. Second, how one ought to act politically is determined by the theory of practical ethics or practical reason. Since Keynes was a consequentialist in this area, and since he took the uncertainty of the future seriously, this meant acting so as to increase the amount of *probable* goodness in the world; or, expressed more carefully, acting so as to bring into existence such a combination of the preconditions to goodness as would probably maximize the amount of goodness that is possible under the circumstances.

Keynes never specified the full range of the preconditions of goodness, but it is not difficult to construct a list of the main items from his and Moore's writings. The underlying principle was set out in *Principia Ethica:* 'anything which hinders [persons] from devoting their energy to the attainment of positive goods seems plainly bad as means ' (1903, p.157). Put positively, this becomes the proposition that anything which facilitates the devotion of energy to the attainment of intrinsic value is good as means. Moore himself mentioned rules directed towards the prevention of murder, the protection of private property, the encouragement of industry, promise-keeping, health and temperance (in the sense of moderation), and the maintenance of freedom (1903, pp. 157, 167, 186). To this initial set may be added four other important items drawn from Keynes's writings:

1.   a solution to the economic problem (understood as the satisfaction of 'absolute needs' and the abolition of 'the struggle for subsistence') (IX, 326–7),
2.   peace,
3.   a right population trend (IX, 450), and
4.   economic efficiency (XIX, 639).

This last may legitimately be interpreted from his writings to cover *both* macroeconomic efficiency (practicably low levels of unemployment and inflation, for example) and microeconomic efficiency in both the private and public sectors.

The political implications of Moore's theory of practical reason in *Principia Ethica,* however, tended strongly towards conservatism. Moore argued that because our knowledge is so incomplete as regards cause–effect relationships and as regards the future, we are unable to form rational beliefs about the future consequences of actions. He then drew *two* conclusions concerning the principles by which individuals should decide what to do. The first, and more important one was that rules which were both 'generally useful and generally practised' in society should always be obeyed, individuals *never* being justified in breaking them. This proposition, highly supportive of the status quo, was antithetical to programmes of social change and reform. The second conclusion was that in situations *not* covered by such rules, individuals were to be guided where possible by direct judgements concerning the goodness of the effects and the probabilities of their attainment. Although it is relegated to a secondary role in comparison to observance of generally practised and generally useful rules, the presence of this second, often overlooked case in Moore's theory is important.

How, then, did Keynes, without abandoning consequentialism and the essential propositions of Moore's theoretical ethics, manage to derive a theory of practical reason that could justify individual judgements, so-called 'immoralism' (X, 446–7) and even political radicalism? It is here that Keynes's theory of probability, set out in his early papers, his fellowship dissertations of 1907 and 1908, and his *Treatise on Probability* of 1921, becomes important in two ways. First, Keynes substituted his own logical theory of probability for the frequency theory upon which Moore had apparently relied. On the logical theory, rational degrees of belief about future consequences do exist, such degrees of belief being expressed by probability-relations between propositions which may be known by means of intellectual intuition. Secondly, Keynes's principle of indifference was deployed to neutralize the effects of an infinite future, ignorance of which played a vital role in leading Moore to his conservative conclusions. If we know absolutely nothing about the remote future, the principle allows remote events to be disregarded in deciding rational action. It thus prevents nescience from paralysing individual judgement, and removes an important support from the justification of Moore's recourse to rule-following. These two developments within probability theory allowed Keynes to reconstruct Moore's consequentialism in a way which liberated individual judgement from unconditional subjugation to generally practised and generally useful rules, and which put the possibility of social change back on the main agenda. Not that Keynes treated rules with disdain. The situation was rather that there was an inversion of priorities. The domain of individual judgement which had taken a secondary position in Moore's account was elevated by Keynes to the main philosophical tribunal. Rules were still respected as socially useful and necessary, but their validity in given circumstances was always open to revision by this higher tribunal.[6]

We thus arrive at Keynes's fundamental conception of political theory and practice. *Politics is the application of ethical theory to policy questions. As a branch of practical reason, its central focus is on (consequentialist) determinations of the most rational course of action under given circumstances.* Its prime concern is thus with the provision of reasons for actions, not with analyses of power, class, social conflict, political structures and institutions. These are not excluded, but obtain their relevance from their bearing on the central question of rational decision-making. From this conception derive certain salient characteristics of his political writings – the never-ceasing appeal to reason, and the view that reason is the most powerful force in politics *in the long run.* Although this valorization of reason has struck many as naively incomplete, it is a direct corollary of Keynes's Moorean framework.

In addition, a fundamental characteristic of Keynes's approach to large political questions is a structure in which the discussion is organized along two axes, the *economic* and the *ethical,* a duality reflecting his means–ends framework, his twin academic concerns with ethics and economics, and his conception of economics as a 'moral science'. The economic axis, sometimes discussed in terms of 'technique' or 'business', is essentially concerned with efficiency in attaining economic ends. The ethical axis, discussion of which is sometimes cast in terms of morality, psychology, religion or 'creed', is concerned with values and intrinsic goodness. This twofold structure is particularly clear in Keynes's assessment of different social systems, but it is also evident elsewhere. It indicates an important dual concern in his politics with the material *and* the spiritual.

Burke's secondary influence
The notion of politics as 'a doctrine of means' received an important additional reinforcement as a result of Keynes's late 1904 study of the famous eighteenth century conservative, Edmund Burke. In a long essay seeking to analyse Burke's political philosophy as a coherent whole still possessing contemporary

relevance, Keynes saw Burke's 'great discovery' to be the proposition that the science of politics was a doctrine of means and not of ends. This meshed perfectly with Keynes's pre-existing Moorean framework. Burke's attack on the notion of abstract rights and ideal forms of government, notions encouraged by the French Revolution, was 'of the utmost importance for all clear and rational thinking on questions of government'.

Keynes also strongly endorsed another of Burke's propositions, his principle of extreme timidity in 'introducing present evil for the sake of future benefits'.

> Our power of prediction is so slight, our knowledge of remote consequences so uncertain, that it is seldom wise to sacrifice a present benefit for a doubtful advantage in the future. Burke ever held, and held rightly, that it can seldom be right to sacrifice the well-being of a nation for a generation, to plunge whole communities in distress, or to destroy a beneficent institution for the sake of a supposed millennium in the comparatively remote future. We can never know enough to make the chance worth taking and the fact that cataclysms in the past have sometimes inaugurated lasting benefits is no argument for cataclysms in general. These fellows, says Burke, have 'gloried in making a Revolution, as if revolutions were good things in themselves' (Keynes, 1904).

This principle is of great significance in Keynes's thought in general, and his politics in particular. It is a corollary to his own theory of practical reason and underlies his long-standing opposition to revolutionary upheavals of society. But while Burke's own tendency was sometimes to oppose all forms of social change, in Keynes's hands the principle was directed only at 'violent' methods of progress. Keynes opposed change which ushered in certain evil in the present in the hope of far greater good in an uncertain future; he was not against reforms in general.

But while admiring much in Burke, Keynes also rejected a great deal – specifically, those parts of Burke which ran counter to Keynes's Moorean foundations and which helped support Burke's extreme conservatism. Worthy of particular mention here are:

1. Burke's preference for peace over truth, a sentiment utterly opposed to Keynes's quest for truth.
2. Burke's disbelief in the individual's ability to judge rightly in questions of action, a view in direct opposition to Keynes's emerging philosophy of practical reason.
3. Burke's reliance in argument on what was 'natural', which led him 'into more than one fallacious position', including 'very nearly the worst argument ever used' in defence of economic *laissez-faire*.[7]
4. Burke's arguments relating to the distribution of income and wealth, which prompted Keynes to describe his opposition to any schemes of

redistribution and public charity as 'wholly inadequate'.

5.   Burke's conservatism as regards social change, criticized by Keynes as timidity verging on 'absurdity'.
6.   Burke's alarming inconsistencies regarding the principle of toleration, a principle Keynes supported as generally true.

One final question which Burke raised, however, was to engage Keynes for the rest of his life – where to draw the line between the public and private spheres. On this difficult issue, Burke found that he could find no unwavering line, although his own views always tended towards non-interference. And while Keynes's boundary allowed for far greater state activity, he was constantly preoccupied with determining practical solutions to this fundamental problem. As he put it in *The End of Laissez-Faire* of 1924–26: 'We cannot therefore settle on abstract grounds, but must handle *on its merits in detail* what Burke termed "one of the finest problems in legislation, namely, to determine what the State ought to take upon itself to direct..., and what it ought to leave, with as little interference as possible, to individual exertion" '(IX, 288, emphasis added).[8]

The ultimate end

In *Principia Ethica,* Moore declared that 'the rational ultimate end of human action and the sole criterion of social progress' was the bringing into existence of as much intrinsic goodness as possible. 'The only possible reason that can justify any action is that by it the greatest possible amount of what is good absolutely should be realised' (1903, pp.101, 189). The maximization of intrinsic goodness was thus the ultimate end of practical reason, towards which all means to goodness could contribute. Keynes's philosophy adopted the same basic stance, as his unpublished and published writings indicate.[9] (It is worth noting in passing that Burke's ultimate end differed from Keynes's, for Burke's final goal was the peace, comfort and happiness of the people. Nevertheless, since the means which encouraged Burke's end could also encourage Keynes's, Keynes could absorb various lessons from parts of Burke's writings.)

The chief intrinsic goods to which Moore drew attention fell under the two heads of *personal affection* and *aesthetic enjoyment.* These were not the only goods but they included ' *all* the greatest, and *by far* the greatest, goods we can imagine' (1903, p.189, emphasis in original). Though Moore did not specify their contents in detail, both may be interpreted broadly. Personal affection comprises the many forms of love and positive regard in relations between people – friends, parents and children, lovers, spouses and so on – while aesthetic enjoyment encompasses the various forms of beauty – physical, spiritual, artistic, natural, architectural and so forth. Both categories gave rise to the states of consciousness that Moore and Keynes thought essential to intrinsic goodness.[10]

The ultimate goal to which politics and economics were means was thus the creation of an ethically rational society, a 'utopia' characterized by increasing amounts of intrinsic goodness. 'We were', Keynes reminisced in 1938, 'among the last of the Utopians, ...who believe in a continuing moral progress' (X, 447). No blueprint for the ideal society was provided, however, although there is enough in Keynes's various writings to suggest its main features. Clearly it would be a world in which love and beauty, in their many forms, predominated. Between nations, peace and co-operation would replace war, while between individuals, friendship and affection would prevail over hostility and antagonism. Beauty would be both created and preserved. Painting, sculpture, music and theatre would flourish, the natural environment would be protected from despoiling development and pollution, and historical monuments would be maintained. While money would still be used as a means of exchange, money-love or the acquisitive obsession with money for its own sake would disappear. Purposiveness, in the sense of the postponement of enjoyment to a never-arriving future, would decline and with it the motive for high levels of saving. Individuals would increase goodness in the present by plucking 'the hour and the day virtuously and well', and by taking 'direct enjoyment in things' (IX, 331). In the words of *My Early Beliefs* (which tended rather misleadingly to telescope the future into the present), the human race would consist of 'reliable, rational, decent people, influenced by truth and objective standards, who can be safely released from the outward restraints of convention and traditional standards and inflexible rules of conduct, and left ... to their own sensible devices, pure motives and reliable intuitions of the good' (X, 447).

Keynes's ethical ideal was not a stationary state, however. Having no foreseeable upper limit, intrinsic goodness could always be increased. And, facing an uncertain future with finite social and natural scientific knowledge, society would be obliged to rely on rational *experimentation* and learning by doing. What was in view was not a completed Utopia, but an unfinished one forever striving towards further progress and higher levels of civilization.

The journey to the ideal
Naturally, Keynes knew none of this would happen by itself. Two fundamental changes were necessary, one termed economic (though political–economic might be a better description), the other moral or psychological (IX, 293). The first was regarded as easier, the second as far more formidable. As he put it in 1934:

> The economic problem is not too difficult to solve. If you will leave that to me, I will look after it. But when I have solved it, I shall not receive, or deserve, much thanks.

> For I shall have done no more than disclose that the real problem lying behind is quite different and further from solution than before. (XXVIII, 34; also XXVII, 385–6).

The same notion of successively confronting these two problems informed his writings from the 1920s to the 1940s. In 1922, economists were portrayed as 'not only useful but necessary' because they could provide individuals with 'a good house' within whose walls could be collected 'the other ingredients of a good life' (XVII, 432). The 1931 preface to *Essays in Persuasion* set out Keynes's hope and belief that

> ... the day is not far off when the economic problem will take the back seat where it belongs, and that the arena of the heart and head will be occupied, or reoccupied, by *our real problems* – the problems of life and of human relations, of creation and behaviour and religion (IX, xviii, emphasis added).

The same twofold theme emerged in his general policy stance of 1937:

> The natural evolution should be towards a decent level of consumption for everyone; and, when that is high enough, towards the occupation of our energies in the non-economic interests of our lives. Thus we need to be slowly reconstructing our social system with these ends in view (XXI, 393).

And it underlay his 1943 House of Lords speech:

> ... to make a bogey of the economic problem is, in my judgement, grievously to misunderstand the nature of the tasks ahead of us. ...The real problems of the future are first of all the maintenance of peace, of international cooperation and amity, and beyond that the profound moral and social problems of how to organise material abundance to yield up the fruits of a good life (XXVII, 260–1).

The first, economic, change involved the establishment and growth of various of the preconditions of goodness. Basically this meant the widespread dissemination of material comfort and economic security on the one hand, and of leisure time on the other. Love and beauty could obviously only be fully enjoyed by those who have time and who are free of economic insecurity. Generating both these conditions naturally required *efficiency* in production, not only in terms of technology and institutional practices, but also in macroeconomic, microeconomic and international terms. It also required population growth to be on a sustainable path in relation to technology and the environment; sufficient abundance of time, output and natural beauty cannot be provided until the Malthusian devil is chained up. As regards the *pace of change*, four main determinants were isolated – population control, avoidance of armed conflict, the willingness to be legitimately guided by science (including presumably, economics), and the rate of accumulation (IX, 331).

The solution to the economic problem was so important that Keynes was prepared, in the interests of facilitating its accomplishment, to tolerate an inversion of certain values for a limited period. Economically, various injustices and evils were to be broadly accepted in the short term because of their usefulness in promoting the accumulation of capital and in laying the necessary foundations.

> For at least another hundred years we must pretend to ourselves and to everyone that fair is foul and foul is fair; for foul is useful and fair is not. Avarice and usury and precaution must be our gods for a little longer still. *For only they can lead us out of the tunnel of economic necessity into daylight* (IX, 331, emphasis added).

In the economic domain, usefulness or expediency could thus temporarily subdue moral values in the interests of longer term ethical rationality. But once the economic battle was over, individuals would be able to 'devote their energies to non-economic purposes', to 'matters of greater and more permanent significance' (IX, 326, 332).

> ... for the first time since his creation man will be faced with his real, his permanent problem – how to use his freedom from pressing economic cares, how to occupy his leisure, which science and compound interest will have won for him, to live wisely and agreeably and well.
>
> The strenuous purposeful money-makers may carry all of us along with them into the lap of economic abundance. But it will be those peoples, who can keep alive, and cultivate into a fuller perfection, the art of life itself and do not sell themselves for the means of life, who will be able to enjoy the abundance when it comes (IX, 328).

With the economic barrier overcome, there remained the more complex moral-psychological obstacle. This was a problem which Keynes could identify and describe, but on which he uncharacteristically had very little to say as regards remedies. It arose from what I shall term the *domination of money*, a theme emerging in his writings from at least 1924 which was well summed up in 1925.

> ... to me it seems clearer every day that the moral problem of our age is concerned with the love of money, with the habitual appeal to the money motive in nine-tenths of the activities of life, with the universal striving after individual economic security as the prime object of endeavour, with the social approbation of money as the measure of constructive success, and with the social appeal to the hoarding instinct as the foundation of the necessary provision for the family and for the future (IX, 268–9).

The solution required was a 'revolution in our ways of thinking and feeling about money', a revolution which could become 'the growing purpose of contemporary embodiments of the ideal' (IX, 269). With the dictatorship of money overturned, we would then be able

> ... to assess the money-motive at its true value. The love of money as a possession – as distinguished from the love of money as a means to the enjoyment and realities of life – will be recognised for what it is, a somewhat disgusting morbidity, one of those semi-criminal, semi-pathological propensities (IX, 329).

The link between evil and money-love reflected in these remarks is an ancient one, harking back to early Greek and Christian thought. It is related to Keynes's comments on, and attitude towards, 'religion', a word often standing for ethical creed. Money-making, the driving force behind 'absolutely irreligious' capitalism (IX, 267), was 'the grand substitute motive' for those who had 'no creed' (IX, 320). Keynes's atheism naturally did not imply the irrelevance of ethics and values; in a godless universe, an ethical philosophy grounded on human reason was all the more important. Believing an ethical creed to be essential, he often praised many of the moral values advocated by religion, several of which had affinities to the goods and evils of the fount of his own creed, *Principia Ethica*. The importance given to these values (as distinct from theology) is reflected in his vision of the future as allowing a 'return to some of the most sure and certain principles of religion and traditional virtue – that avarice is a vice, that ... usury is a misdemeanour, and the love of money is detestable' (IX, 330–1). The virtue of communism, moreover, resided in its being a 'new religion' which sought to overturn the dominance of money and which might therefore make a valuable contribution to the ideal (IX, 257).

Ridding the world of the domination of money was clearly an immense task. Suppression of the capitalist driving force of money-making meant the transformation of both society and individuals. But while Keynes was clear on the general features of the destination, he had remarkably few thoughts to offer on how to achieve the necessary transformations. The prospect of the transition, in fact, was not one he anticipated with enjoyment.

> ... I think with dread of the readjustment of the habits and instincts of the ordinary man, bred into him for countless generations, which he may be asked to discard within a few decades. ... must we not expect a general 'nervous breakdown'? ... there is no country and no people, I think, who can look forward to the age of leisure and abundance without a dread. For we have been trained too long to strive and not to enjoy (IX, 327–8).

But as usual he remained optimistic, appearing ultimately to base his hopes for successful change on reason and persuasion and on guided, experimental evolution. Nevertheless, the *General Theory's* separation of the tasks of 'transmuting human nature...and of managing it' hints at one aspect of the transition. In the short and medium term, the task was management – to allow the money game to continue but to reduce the stakes and lower economic inequality. As long as 'a significant section of the community [was] strongly addicted to the money-making passion', it could be 'wise and prudent states-manship to allow the game to be played, *subject to rules and limitations*'. But ultimately the goal was transmutation – 'in the ideal commonwealth' individu-als would be 'taught or inspired or bred to take no interest in the stakes' (VII, 374, emphasis added).

Keynes's aversion to money-love is related to several other important themes in his writings. First, it is here that a principal part of Freud's significance for Keynes lies. Freud could be interpreted as having commenced a scientific investigation into the roots of money-love, and as supporting the notion that money-love was not part of human nature but a disease or 'morbid-ity' which could be eliminated in the ideal. Second, it is linked to a host of motifs in his economic writings, including his defence of productive entrepreneurs and industrial capital, his critique of financial capital and 'functionless' rentiers whose euthanasia was envisaged in the *General Theory* (VII, 376), his attacks on excessive thrift, and his attitude towards earned and unearned income. Whereas labour earned its income through effort, interest payments rewarded 'no genuine sacrifice' (VII, 376). Third, Keynes was aware he was resurrecting a medieval religious attitude to the interest rate and the need for intervention to prevent its tendency to rise to usurious levels (VII, 351–2). [11] Fourth, it is related to his life-long academic fascination with money – its history, its essential characteristics, its economic functions, and its institutions and how they might be reformed. In sum, this preoccupation with money combined with his recon-structed version of *Principia Ethica* exerted a profound influence over the framework and orientation of his political and social analysis.

Capitalism
Explicitly or implicitly, conventional portraits present Keynes as the inten-tional saviour of capitalism, a reformer seeking modification for purposes of permanently preserving this form of economic organization. Galbraith, himself a Keynesian, views Keynes as being convinced that 'capitalism was worth saving, that it could be made to work' and as being 'exceedingly comfortable with the economic system he so brilliantly explored' (1985, pp. 58, 60). Further to the left, Hunt (1979, pp. 377, 384, 395) depicts Keynes as 'one of the most brilliant conservative economists of this century' whose goal was 'to save capitalism from self-destruction'. [12] The conventional picture, however, is badly incomplete and misleading. While certainly seeking to maintain wisely managed forms of capitalism in the short and medium term, Keynes was very much concerned with the long term abolition of capitalism as he conceived it. His ultimate goal was a non-capitalist, ethically rational utopia, whose charac-teristics resembled more closely those of communist or left-wing utopias than

those based on free market or right-wing ideals. (One ought also to bear in mind that Keynes always firmly rejected *laissez-faire* or individualistic capitalism, and advocated wisely supervised capitalism with an interventionist state; *laissez-faire,* in his view, had been effective in the nineteenth century but was no longer appropriate to the altered conditions of the twentieth.)

Of capitalism, Keynes had an unconventional, non-Marxist conception, defining it in terms of *the dominance of money.* '[W]hat seems to me to be the essential characteristic of capitalism', he wrote in 1924–26, '[is] the dependence upon an intense appeal to the money-making and money-loving instincts of individuals as the main motive force of the economic machine' (IX, 293). Coming from a Moorean philosopher this was not surprising, for money-making and money-love could easily be identified as among the chief forces deflecting individuals from the pursuit of intrinsic goodness. Making fortunes might be defensible in terms of economic rationality, but obsession with money subverted the achievement of the higher form of ethical rationality. The conception underlay Keynes's animus towards the Benthamite tradition. Based 'on an over-valuation of the economic criterion', it was excoriated in 1938 as 'the worm ... gnawing at the insides of modern civilisation' causing 'its present moral decay' and 'destroying the quality of the popular Ideal' (X, 445–6).

From this conception flowed the two basic elements of Keynes's attitude toward capitalism, an attitude not dissimilar to those of left-wing critiques. On *economic* grounds capitalism was praised as the most efficient of existing systems for the attainment of economic ends. But on *ethical or moral* grounds, it was 'in many ways extremely objectionable' (X, 294). The money motive, combined with wise state supervision, could generate high economic efficiency, but at the same time it rendered capitalism incapable of directly and substantially enhancing intrinsic goodness. Capitalism's task was to develop the productive forces of society to establish some of the preconditions of goodness. But over time the intense appeal to the money motive that epitomized capitalism for Keynes was to be gradually controlled and marginalized until it was eliminated as a socially dominant force. With its demise, individuals would then be free to occupy themselves in ways which increased intrinsic goodness.

While Keynes's conception of capitalism differed greatly from Marx's, there are nevertheless some affinities. Like Keynes, Marx viewed capitalism as a money-economy, functioning through the M–C–M' relationship (money–commodities–money) rather than the simple circulation of C–M–C (commodities–money–commodities).[13] Marx also portrayed capitalists as dominated by the imperatives of expanding money and wealth. Motivated by a 'boundless greed after riches,' a 'passionate chase after exchange-value', the capitalist, *qua* capitalist, aimed not at obtaining use-values but solely at the 'restless never-ending process of profit-making'.[14] The elimination of capitalism in Keynes's sense would thus also be a consequence of the overthrow of capitalism in Marx's. In attaining their respective ideals, moreover, there is a related movement from a realm of necessity to a realm of freedom.

Communism

Despite his finding much to object to in the new Soviet system, communism had a special significance for Keynes. On the economic side, it was viewed as highly inefficient, the only bright spots being some prospects for improvement and a healthy reliance on experimentation which was of 'high interest' to the West (XIX, 441). Ethically, too, it was criticized for its suppression of individual liberty. But on the ethical side it possessed an enormous virtue which capitalism intrinsically lacked. By seeking 'a framework of society in which pecuniary motives ... shall have a changed relative importance', it challenged the domination of money. The '*emotional and ethical essence*' of Leninism, he emphatically declared in 1925, centred upon '*the individual's and the community's attitude towards the love of money* (IX, 259, emphasis in original). A form of society in which it was even partially true that the life calculations of rational individuals were not based on money-making and money-accumulating was, he thought, 'a tremendous innovation' (IX, 261). In attempting a 'revolution in our ways of thinking and feeling about money', the Soviet Union was conducting a most significant experiment in life's moral laboratory. This was something which the very nature of capitalism prevented. Thus despite the cruelty and stupidity, Soviet communism had touched upon something 'partly true, or sympathetic to the souls of modern men'. It was thus turned towards 'the possibilities of things' and might yet uncover 'some speck of the ideal'.

Keynes's political position

That Keynes was a liberal there can be little doubt. It is evident from his political writings, as well as his own declarations. As he remarked in 1934, 'My own aim is economic reform by the methods of political liberalism' (XXVIII, 29).[15] What is more intriguing, however, is the *nature* of his liberalism. My contention here is that it is a distinctive form of liberalism whose centre of gravity is left of centre. This is consistent with his philosophical formation which provided a Moorist conception of the ultimate end of rational action, and a theory of practical reason capable of justifying social change. Achieving Moore's ideal clearly required *massive* transformations of existing capitalist society and forms of individual behaviour. It is this which gives Keynes's politics much of its left or radical edge. But it was very much a liberal, non-Marxist leftism. With the goodness that was to be maximized residing in mental states, the emphasis was firmly upon respect for individuals. Combined with a theory of practical reason which aimed at augmenting existing goodness and legislated against introducing large evils in the present in order to gain hypothetical goodness in the distant future, the political thrust was towards non-revolutionary means of transformation. As he put it in 1939, 'it is only on lines of liberalism that there can be peaceful, non-violent evolution of social and economic institutions' (XXI, 493). Reasoned experimentation was to govern the nature and rate of social change, not violent, widespread upheavals. In addition, the main appeal made by Keynes's politics was not to class, or to the winning of strategic capital–labour conflicts, but to reason and the intelligence of individuals regardless of their class background. As a result, it saw itself as open to alliances of like-minded individuals, inclusive of humane conservatives, progressive liberals and non-fundamentalist socialists.

Conservatism
Of conservatism as a political doctrine relevant to the twentieth century, Keynes was never an exponent. His cutting remarks of 1925 typified his general stance.

> How could I bring myself to be a Conservative? They offer me neither food nor drink – neither intellectual nor spiritual consolation. ...[It] promotes neither my self-interest nor the public good. It leads nowhere; it satisfies no ideal; it conforms to no intellectual standard; it is not even safe, or calculated to preserve from spoilers that degree of civilisation which we have already attained (IX, 296–7).

Whereas nineteenth century conservatism had been progressive and appropriate to the times, contemporary conservatism faced major problems. First, it was historically outmoded – it had 'not a vestige of a plan or an idea for the new problems of today' (XIX, 648). Second, it failed to embrace continuing reform, being 'more concerned to prevent backsliding' than to promote further progress (VI, 268). And thirdly, it tended to be a home for 'die-hards' who, like fundamentalists on the left, saw politics in terms of 'capitalism *versus* socialism', and meant to 'die in the last ditch for capitalism' (IX, 310, emphasis in original). However, to conservatism in the non-political sense of seeking where possible the preservation of things of value bequeathed by the past, Keynes was very much attracted. Given his theory of practical reason, it was only natural that he could describe his thought as 'moderately conservative in its implications' (VII, 377), and as combining 'an unlimited readiness to experiment' in economics and politics with 'a sort of careful conservatism, thrifty of everything which has human experience behind it' (XXVIII, 334) .

Liberalism
Keynes's distinctive form of liberalism, which envisaged significant domains for both individualism and state activity, placed him firmly in the ranks of left liberalism. After being instrumental in the 1923 takeover of the *Nation,* he stated his fundamental position in its foreword of 5 May:

Our own sympathies are for a Liberal Party which has its centre well to the left, a party definitely of change and progress, discontented with the world, striving after many things; but with bolder, freer, more disinterested minds than Labour has, and quit of their out-of-date dogmas. We should like to play a part in forming and expressing the new thoughts of the world, ... and in building something to which enthusiasm is appropriate, and which is based on firm foundations of reason and good sense (XVIII, 125).

But to fulfil this role, the Liberal party had to adapt and modernize its political philosophy, it had to abandon the *laissez-faire* thrust of old liberalism and develop new ideas and policies capable of generating further social improvement. 'The Liberal Party', he contended in 1926, 'should be not less progressive than Labour, not less open to new ideas, not behindhand in constructing the new world' (IX, 311). To emancipate the Liberals from 'the dead wood of the past' (IX, 300), and to see the emergence of 'a reformed and remodelled Liberalism' (XIX, 441) were his goals. This new form of liberalism would be applicable to the altered conditions of the post-1918 world and would facilitate the evolution of society along the lines of his ethical philosophy.

But even if armed with such a new philosophy, the post-1918 Liberal Party was far too small to win power, a fact which made the idea of alliances between progressives of all parties very attractive to Keynes. Given the small number of 'humane' Tories, co-operation between Liberals and Labour provided the best opportunities. Labour possessed the necessary electoral base and a strong commitment to social justice, while the Liberals brought a defence of individual freedom and the intellectual resources to ensure that social reforms would be 'sound' and 'enduring'. In this way, a solution could be found to the 'political problem of mankind', defined by Keynes as a combination of 'three things: economic efficiency, social justice and individual liberty' (IX, 311). Labour underpinned the second ingredient, the Liberals the first and third. Naturally, as well as changes in the Liberal Party, such co-operation required that moderate, rather than radical socialism prevailed within the Labour Party. Within such alliances, however, Keynes was concerned to retain the unique identity of the Liberals, and opposed fusion with the Labour Party.[16]

In discussing Keynes's liberalism, however, one of the trickiest issues is identifying his relationship to 'New Liberalism', a movement which flourished in Britain from the 1870s to 1914. New Liberalism represented a significant leftward shift among liberals. It rejected old or *laissez-faire* liberalism, emphasized the social nature of individuals, advocated collectivism and significant state activity, and possessed a strong commitment to social justice.[17] Recent discussion is sharply divided on the question as to whether Keynes was or was not a New Liberal. Clarke (1978, p.132; 1983, pp.175–7) argues he clearly was, Freeden (1986, pp.15, 154–73) that he clearly was not. My contention is that this is a false polarisation because no unequivocal answer exists to the question posed by the debate; it is therefore far more constructive to reorient the discussion towards an investigation of the various areas of coincidence and rupture between Keynes and New Liberalism.

Such investigation reveals two essential points. First, as regards *conclusions,* there is considerable overlap between many (but not all) of the ideas reached by New Liberalism and Keynes. These similarities underpin Clarke's argument. But second, as regards *foundations,* there are various profound differences between Keynes and New Liberalism. Freeden's argument draws upon some of these, though many important ones escape through his neglect of Moore. The foundations of New Liberalism were laid by philosophers such as T.H. Green, D.G. Ritchie and L.T. Hobhouse and economists like J.A. Hobson, intellectuals whose influences on Keynes during the relevant periods were either non-existent, minimal or even negative. Keynes's philosophical and economic foundations were entirely different. In philosophy he was moulded primarily by Moore and Russell, and in economics by Marshall.[18] It is these significant differences which complicate the discussion and put simple answers out of reach.

The bearing that Keynes's philosophical foundations have on the debate may be illustrated with the important issue of *social justice.* Freeden argues that Keynes, in his overriding pursuit of economic efficiency, relegated social justice and distribution to relative insignificance. This is an unbalanced picture which helps lead Freeden to the mistaken conclusion that Keynes was not a left liberal but a 'centrist-liberal, if not slightly to the right of that' (1986, p.171). While issues of social justice and questions of distribution were certainly not as dominant for Keynes as they were for New Liberalism, they were nevertheless genuine and important concerns throughout several decades. In 1925 he explicitly advocated the control of economic forces 'in the interests of social justice' (IX, 305), while in 1927 he set 'a dual aim before the statesman – a society which is just and a society which is efficient' (XIX, 639). The *General Theory* identified the *two* outstanding faults of capitalism to be employment inefficiency and distributional inequality (VII, 372), while his proposals in *How to Pay for the War* were 'conceived in a spirit of social justice' (IX, 373). Keynes never argued for complete egalitarianism, however, only for less inequality than that currently existing. But from this, and the fact that redistribution was never for Keynes the *primary* cure for economic malaise as it was for many New Liberals, it does not follow that it was insignificant in his scheme. The key to his priorities lies in his ethical philosophy and in his economic analysis. Both efficiency and justice were important, but efficiency had the greater contribution to make in the short and medium term regarding progress towards the ideal society. Solving the economic problem was an essential precondition of movement towards the ideal, so it took priority. And while distribution might play supportive roles in his economic analysis, it never played a *central* role in his analysis of, or policy prescriptions for, capitalism. Social justice had to be taken into account while the economic problem was being solved, but for the short and medium term we might have to pretend that 'fair is foul and foul is fair' (IX, 331). However, when 'the tunnel of economic necessity' was passed, the turn of social justice would arrive. Then we shall 'be free, at last, to discard' all kinds of 'economic practices, affecting the distribution of wealth ... which we now maintain at all costs, however, distasteful and unjust they may be in themselves' (IX, 329). To sum up: economic efficiency and social justice were both important political goals, but justice had temporarily to cede priority to efficiency because of the latter's greater contribution to establishing the preconditions of goodness. Once these preconditions were in place, social justice could then occupy its rightful and prominent position.

Socialism

Understanding the sense in which Keynes may be associated with the socialist tradition requires disengagement from a range of Marxist conceptions. Presenting itself as the bearer of true or 'scientific' socialism, Marxism has so powerfully dominated the academic discussion of socialism that non-Marxist socialisms have been relegated to the shadows. Yet socialism has always historically been a broader current of thought than Marxism.

To traditional concepts of socialism, based on class and state ownership, Keynes was always hostile. One who described Marxism as 'illogical' (IX, 285), the economic struggle between classes as ' an *unnecessary* muddle' (IX, xviii, emphasis in original), and nationalisation as 'unimportant' and 'irrelevant' (IX, 290) could hardly have been their advocate. In terms similar to his rejection of political conservatism, he criticized state socialism as an outmoded doctrine inapplicable to modern conditions – it was 'little better than a dusty survival of a plan to meet the problems of fifty years ago' which missed 'the significance of what is actually happening' (IX, 290). However, being opposed to state socialism did not mean Keynes was opposed to all variants of socialism. As he put it in 1923, 'I differ from [Labour] *not* in the desirability of state action in the common interest, but as to *the forms* which such interference should take. ... It is our duty to think out wise controls and workable interferences' (XIX, 159, emphasis added). The *General Theory* also makes plain his rejection of Marxist-inspired socialism and his sympathies with the 'anti-Marxian socialism' of Gesell (VII, 355).[19]

Keynes's advocacy was of a different form of socialism, one based on a combination of social control and individualism. In 1939 he christened it 'liberal socialism'.

> ... by [liberal socialism] I mean a system where we can act as an organised community for common purposes and to promote social and economic justice,

whilst respecting and protecting the individual – his freedom of choice, his faith, his mind and its expression, his enterprise and his property (XXI, 500).

It harked back to his earlier 1924 notion of the 'true socialism of the future' which would emerge 'from co-operation between private initiative and the public exchequer' and 'from an endless variety of experiments directed towards discovering the respective appropriate spheres of the individual and the social, and the terms of fruitful alliance between these sister instincts' (XIX, 222). The historic antithesis between capitalism and socialism was regarded as a false antagonism, the sensible way forward under present conditions being an 'amalgam of private capitalism and state socialism' (XXI, 492). Thought and experiment were capable of devising policies and institutions which retained the main advantages and discarded the main deficiencies of each.

Keynes never spelled out in one place the main principles of 'liberal socialism', but an informative account can nevertheless be gleaned from his prolific output. It was 'liberal' in the sense that it protected and fostered a broad field for individualism – not *laissez-faire* individualism, but an individualism in which as wide a variety of personal freedoms existed as was consistent with the social good. Freedoms of expression were high on the list, but freedom of enterprise and private property were also defended. And it was 'socialist' in that the state, as the representative of society as a whole, was the guardian, manager and promoter of a rational, civilized society. Its main tasks were to remedy the considerable deficiencies of unrestricted individualism, to create the preconditions of goodness, and to facilitate the attainment of higher levels of ethical rationality. Keynes's conception of socialism did not repose on an economic criterion of public ownership of the means of production, or on a social justice criterion of distributional equality. The sense in which his stance was socialist rested on broader criteria. It aimed, like other socialisms, at constructing a morally superior society; and it sought, via the state and its ancillary institutions, to exercise significant social control over society's development.

In Keynes's scheme, the state's agenda largely depended upon the performance of the private sector in establishing the preconditions of goodness. This gave it an interest in a vast range of issues – economic efficiency, leisure time, social justice, population, education, the arts, peace, and the natural environment, for example. A wide range of state activities was sanctioned – the provisions of practicably low unemployment and inflation rates using all economic policy instruments according to circumstances, the elimination of extreme distributional inequalities, support for artistic endeavour, environmental protection, and the development of data collection agencies, to name but a few. *Planning* was also an essential state function, not fully centralized planning, but planning in the sense of controls over, and strategic interventions into, an economy composed of otherwise freely interacting units. As he put it in 1932, it is of the essence of state planning to do those things which ... lie outside the scope of the individual. ... Its object is to take hold of the central controls and to govern them with deliberate foresight and thus modify and condition the environment within which the individual freely operates (XXI, 88).

As well as activities directed from the centre (such as a National Investment Board), Keynes also favoured 'the growth ... of semi-autonomous bodies' within the public sector in the belief that the 'ideal size for the unit of control and organisation lies somewhere between the individual and the modern State' (IX, 288). The difference between Keynes's and some of the more traditional socialisms is encapsulated in the contrast between the *socialization* of investment which he advocated (VII, 378), and the general *nationalization* of industry which he rejected. The former meant bringing the volume, and partly the direction, of investment under social control, whereas the latter meant involving the state in the economy more than was either necessary or desirable. But while Keynes favoured significant state control, it is worth noting that there is nothing in his writings to support the proposition that bigger government is necessarily better government. In keeping with his consequentialism, the size and scope of state activity was a matter for judgement based on the merits and circumstances of the case. And whatever the overall size of the state sector, efficiency in its various operations was an important concern. The state, in Keynes's scheme, was thus far more than a neutral umpire preserving an existing capitalist society; it was an active manager with an ethically based programme of social reform and evolutionary change. At bottom, Keynes's liberal socialism rejected inevitable oppositions between capitalism and socialism, between democracy and planning, between individualism and state intervention. What it sought were new modes of economic and political organization combining the best in all these worlds.[20]

In Keynes's view, *both* liberalism and socialism had rationally to adapt to changed historical circumstances. Ideas and policies developed in earlier periods were to be replaced by new conceptions appropriate to altered conditions. With each more open to the valuable elements of the other, liberalism and socialism could combine into a powerful and progressive political force capable of supervising major evolutionary social transformations.

Keynes's review of Clissold
Read as political allegory, Keynes's widely overlooked 1927 review of H. G. Wells's *The World of William Clissold* (IX, 315–20) yields the following instructive overview of his political stance. Rather than remain inactive, we should encourage movement to something better. But 'whence is to come the motive power of desirable change?' Conservatism is woefully inadequate because of its 'folly of looking backwards' and the 'danger of inadaptability'. However, intelligent people are also disillusioned with Socialism – 'sentimen-

talists and pseudo-intellectuals' with good feelings but wrong ideas cannot carry off the necessary 'constructive revolution'. The revolutionaries who will actually lead us 'far, far to the Left' are to be found elsewhere, among the creative intellectuals currently devoting themselves primarily to science and business. Their energies can be harnessed by liberalism, but first 'political Liberalism must die to be born again' with a clearer philosophy. A creed could then replace the empty motive of money-making, and the practical business-man and the 'active and constructive temperaments in every political camp' could become 'apostles'. The union of Siva and Brahma, of the justified but potentially destructive creative passions of labour and of the creative intelli-gence of liberals, will create a new political force capable of setting in train changes which will enable us to 'begin to reap spiritual fruits from our material conquests'.

Conclusion

It is claimed that the *conceptual framework* advanced in this chapter discloses, for the first time, the philosophical foundations necessary to the full under-standing of Keynes's politics. This framework satisfactorily meets the critical test of generating an account consistent with *all* of Keynes's political, eco-nomic and social writings and not just some of them, a test which finds alternative interpretations wanting. It is thus able to make sense of a variety of remarks which otherwise seem puzzling or eccentric, and, in particular, is able to assist in pinning down the elusive variants of liberalism and socialism to which Keynes adhered. In advancing this framework, no attempt has been made to offer a complete account of Keynes's politics, for that is a task that would take an entire book.

Nor is any claim entered that Keynes is a major political philosopher. Nevertheless the investigation of his politics is important for two reasons. First, Keynes is one of the intellectual giants of the twentieth century whose thought has directly or indirectly moulded Western society, and the politics of this political economist, having resisted many attempts at analysis, are in urgent need of clarification. Second, while he may not have achieved greatness as a political thinker, his political writings nevertheless contain important lessons. Leaving evident weaknesses aside, Keynes's political legacy may be summed up in two broad propositions – the attempt to make politics the servant of an ethical vision in which both the material and the spiritual are significant, and the attempt to develop an alternative politics based on a specific fusion of liberalism and socialism that is appropriate to twentieth century conditions. While not irrelevant to conservatism, his politics are clearly far more pertinent to those interested in social progress through combinations of liberalism and socialism. Indeed, had the left better understood and utilized Keynes's political insights, it might have been less vulnerable to some of its sharper vicissitudes. In the current climate of re-evaluation, it may even yet draw benefits from a serious consideration of Keynes's alternative programme.

Notes

1. A paper presented to the 1989 HES Conference, Richmond, Virginia, and to the 1989 HETSA Conference, Canberra, Australia. I would like to thank participants at both conferences for their comments, as well as King's College, Cambridge for permission to quote from the Keynes Papers, and the Australian Research Council for assistance with funding.
2. Most of Keynes's published political writings are to be found in volumes IX, XIX, XX, XXI and XXVIII of the *Collected Writings of John Maynard Keynes*, with other important comments scattered through the remaining volumes. References to the *Collected Writings* take the form of the volume number followed by the page number(s).
3. See, for example, Freeden (1986, p. 154): 'In order to reconstruct his political thinking one has to turn to [Keynes's direct writings on politics], as well as attempt to glean political attitudes from some of his specific economic proposals'.
4. For attributions of conservatism, see, for example, Johnson (1974, p.109) and Hunt (1979, ch. 16); for attributions of socialism, see Rowse (1932b) and Hyams (1963, p.125). The secondary literature dealing with Keynes's politics includes Brunner (1987), Clarke (1978, 1983), Cranston (1978), Dillard (1948), Freeden (1986), Holland (1977), Johnson and Johnson (1974), Lambert (1963), Parsons (1983), and Rowse (1932a, 1932b, 1936a, 1936b).
5. For a detailed account of Keynes's theory of practical reason and its consequentialist foundations, see O'Donnell (1982, 1989, ch. 6).
6. For a more detailed account of the issues discussed in the paragraph, see O'Donnell (1989, chs. 1–7).
7. Burke had argued that the laws of commerce are the laws of nature and hence the laws of God. Keynes had no time for such fusions of the social, natural and supernatural.
8. For further discussion of Burke's influence on Keynes, see O'Donnell (1989, pp. 276–85). Skidelsky's (1983, pp.154–7) discussion of Keynes's politics attributes an excessive influence to Burke. This follows from his denial of any connection between Moore's philosophy and Keynes's politics, a denial which obliges recourse to entirely non-Moorean sources such as Burke. It is related to the view, criticized in O'Donnell (1989, pp.114–17), that Moore's philosophy pushed Keynes towards a purely private domain of 'unworldliness', as distinct from the outside realm of public affairs.
9. See, for example, O'Donnell (1989, chs.6,7). One of the earliest commentaries to recognize the importance of ethical ends and a vision of the good society for Keynes was Timlin (1947), a theme latterly taken up by O'Donnell (1982) and Preston (1987).
10. The distinction that Keynes drew in some of his early philosophical papers between the 'goodness' and 'fitness' of objects is relevant but unimportant in the context of this chapter because the distinction belongs to theoretical ethics. So far as practical ethics was concerned Keynes thought that rational action should take both fitness and goodness into consideration; see O'Donnell (1989, ch. 6).
11. For further discussion, see Somerville (1931, 1932, 1936) and Dillard (1948, ch. 12).
12. For additional instances, see Dillard (1948, p.334), Selsam and Wells (1949, p.82), Mattick (1971, ch. 11, p.335), Parsons (1983, pp.381–2), Freeden (1986, p.160 n143).
13. In 1933, on the way to the *General Theory*, Keynes employed an analogy with Marx's M–C–M' schema; see Moggridge (1976, p.104), XIII, 420, XXIX, 81–2.
14. *Capital*, vol I, ch. 4. See also ibid, ch. 24: 'Accumulate, accumulate! That is Moses and the prophets!' For Marx on M–C–M', see *Capital*, vol. I, chs 3,4.
15. Keynes's essay 'Am I a Liberal?' (IX, 295–306) is really concerned with another question, 'What is the nature of my liberalism?' It focuses on some of his political beliefs and his theoretical and practical prescriptions for the Liberal Party. After indicating his own version of liberalism, Keynes then leaves it to his audience, presumably including old

liberals, New Liberals and liberals of his own persuasion, to decide by their own lights the answer to the question posed by his title.

16.   This is evident in his remarks of 1925, used above to illustrate the initially puzzling nature of his politics. His dissatisfaction with Labour also emerges in his 1936 reply to A.L. Rowse who asked why he was not a member of the Labour Party: 'I agree with you that there is, or ought to be, little divergence between the political implications of my ideas and the policy of the Labour Party. I should officially join that Party if it did not seem to be divided between enthusiasts who turn against a thing if there seems a chance that it could possibly happen, and leaders so conservative that there is more to hope from Mr Baldwin' (Keynes Papers, King's College).

17.   For further discussion of New Liberalism, see Bullock and Shock (1956), Emy (1973), Freeden (1978, 1986), Weiler (1982) and Greenleaf (1983).

18.   While Moore wrote next to nothing that bore directly on politics, Russell certainly did. The political philosophy he advanced in 1917 (Russell, 1963) is very similar to Keynes's, though with some differences. Like Keynes, Russell saw politics as a means to goodness and higher levels of civilization. Economic goods were necessary, but 'mental and spiritual goods' were of greater value, these latter depending on individual liberty and creative impulses. Capitalism and state socialism were both criticized, a new system based on a combination of individual freedom and public control being urged. Where Russell differed from Keynes was chiefly in the severity of his critique of capitalism (which was not even viewed as efficient), in his criticisms of power and private property, in his stronger emphasis on democracy (including industrial democracy), and in his sympathies with certain guild socialist ideas. Russell was more impatient in the short term to abolish capitalism and encourage new workplace practices.

Marshall's 'distant goal' was that of an 'ideally perfect social organisation' in which abundance of machinery would reduce working hours and in which 'the opportunities of a noble life' would be accessible to all. Marshall also favoured a (non-Marxist) form of socialism which valued enterprise (1923, pp. vii, viii, 660–5).

Investigation of the connections between the Cambridge Apostles and British espionage cases has revealed further evidence of Keynes's opposition to Marxist socialism. In Keynes's younger years, the Apostles were primarily preoccupied with Cambridge philosophy, but by the 1930s, when Keynes played a diminished role, Marxism was all pervasive. Although he sympathised with the need for reform and respected such individuals as Julian Bell, Keynes strongly opposed the intellectual dominance of Marxism and was critical of Anthony Blunt. In late 1933 and early 1934, Victor Rothschild could write to Keynes: 'We talk endlessly in the Society about Communism which is rather dull. ...I believe I have discovered a fallacy in the whole racket; no doubt you could tell me a hundred. ... The fact is an atmosphere of decadence is appearing and we need your presence' (quoted in Costello, 1988, p.642 n7; see also ibid, chs.10, 14). It is this context of the Marxist capture of the Apostles, I suggest, which provided one of the motivations for the writing of *My Early Beliefs,* and which helps explain some of that document's errors and highly misleading features (on which see O'Donnell, 1989, pp.148–54.)

19.   The future, Keynes thought, would learn more from the spirit of Gesell (if not the letter) than it would from that of Marx. Gesell, who received five pages in the *General Theory,* was of twofold significance for Keynes. First, he was trying to establish an alternative, anti-Marxist socialism based on a repudiation of the foundations of classical or *laissez-faire* doctrine; in Keynes's eccentric view, one of Marxism's major flaws was its acceptance of these theoretical foundations. Secondly, Gesell confronted the problem of money and sought to remove its yoke. Though incomplete, his theoretical and practical ideas on money were nevertheless viewed as containing seeds of advance (VII, 353–8) . For an interesting, early account of Keynes's politics in basic sympathy with that presented here, see Winch's (1969) appendix 'Keynes and the British Left in the Inter-War Period'.

20.   The above overview may be supplemented by the more detailed discussion (with supporting quotations) in O'Donnell (1989), chs. 14, 15.

References

Brunner, R. (1987), 'The Sociopolitical Vision of Keynes', in D.A. Reese (ed.), *The Legacy of Keynes*, San Francisco: Harper and Row.

Bullock, A. and Shock, M. (eds) (1956), *The Liberal Tradition, From Fox to Keynes*, London: Adam & Charles Black.

Clarke, P. (1978), *Liberals and Social Democrats*, Cambridge: Cambridge University Press.

Clarke, P. (1983), 'The Politics of Keynesian Economics, 1924–1931', in M. Bentley and J. Stevenson (eds) *High and Low Politics in Modern Britain*, Oxford: Oxford University Press.

Costello, J. (1988), *Mask of Treachery*, London: Collins.

Cranston, M. (1978), 'Keynes: His Political Ideas and Their Influence', in A.P. Thirlwall (ed.), *Keynes and Laissez-Faire*, London: Macmillan.

Dillard, D. (1948), *The Economics of J.M. Keynes*, New York: Prentice-Hall.

Emy, H.V. (1973), *Liberals, Radicals and Social Politics 1892–1914*, Cambridge: Cambridge University Press.

Freeden, M. (1978), *The New Liberalism*, Oxford: Oxford University Press.

Freeden, M. (1986), *Liberalism Divided*, Oxford: Oxford University Press.

Galbraith, J.K. (1985), 'Keynes, Roosevelt and the Complementary Revolutions', in H.L. Wattel (ed.) *The Policy Consequences of John Maynard Keynes*, Armonk, New York: M.E. Sharpe.

Greenleaf, W.H. (1983), *The British Political Tradition*, vol. 2, London: Methuen.

Helburn, S.W. (1988), 'Keynes and Burke', paper presented to the History of Economics Society Conference, Toronto.

Holland, S. (1977), 'Keynes and the Socialists' in R. Skidelsky (ed.) *The End of the Keynesian Era*, London: Macmillan.

Hunt, E.K. (1979), *History of Economic Thought: A Critical Perspective*, Belmont, California: Wadsworth Publishing Co.

Hyams, E. (1963), *The New Statesman*, London: Longmans.

Johnson, E.S. (1974), 'Scientist or Politician?', *Journal of Political Economy*, **82**, 1, Jan–Feb.

Johnson, E.S. and Johnson, H.G. (1974), 'The Social and Intellectual Origins of the General Theory', *History of Political Economy*, **6**, 3, Autumn.

Keynes, J.M. (1904), 'The Political Doctrines of Edmund Burke', November. Keynes Papers, King's College, Cambridge.

Keynes, J.M. (1905), 'Miscellanea Ethica', July–September. Keynes Papers, King's College, Cambridge.

Keynes, J.M. (1971–1989), *The Collected Writings of John Maynard Keynes*, vols I to XXX, London: Macmillan.

Keynes, J.M. (1921), *Treatise on Probability*. Reprinted in the *Collected Writings of John Maynard Keynes*, Vol. VIII, London: Macmillan.

Keynes, M. (ed.) (1975), *Essays on John Maynard Keynes*, Cambridge University Press.

Lambert, P. (1963), 'The Social Philosophy of John Maynard Keynes', *Annals of Collective Economy*, **34**, 4, October–December.

Marshall, A. (1923), *Industry and Trade*, 4th ed., London: Macmillan.

Marx, K. (1967), *Capital*, vol. I, New York: International Publishers.

Mattick, P. (1971), *Marx and Keynes*, Boston: P. Sargant.

Moggridge, D.E. (1976), *Keynes*, London: Fontana.

Moore, G.E. (1903), *Principia Ethica*, Cambridge: Cambridge University Press.

O'Donnell, R.M. (1982), *Keynes: Philosophy and Economics, An Approach to Rationality and Uncertainty*, PhD dissertation, University of Cambridge.

O'Donnell, R.M. (1989), *Keynes: Philosophy, Economics and Politics*, The Philosophical Foundations of Keynes's Thought and their Influence on his Economics and Politics, London: Macmillan.

Parsons, W. (1983), 'Keynes and the Politics of Ideas', *History of Political Thought*, **4**, (2).

Preston, R.H. (1987), 'The Ethical Legacy of John Maynard Keynes', in D.A. Reese (ed.) *The Legacy of Keynes*, San Francisco: Harper and Row.

Rowse, A.L. (1932a), 'Mr Keynes on Socialism', *The Political Quarterly*, **III**, (3), July–September.

Rowse, A.L. (1932b), 'Socialism and Mr Keynes', *The Nineteenth Century and After*, **112**, September.
Rowse, A.L. (1936a), *Mr Keynes and the Labour Movement*, London: Macmillan.
Rowse, A.L. (1936b), 'Mr Keynes and the Labour Movement', *The Nineteenth Century and After*, **120**, September.
Russell, B. (1963), *Political Ideals*, London: Allen and Unwin. First (American) edition 1917.
Selsam, H. and Wells, H.K. (1949), 'The Philosophy of John Maynard Keynes', *Political Affairs*, February.
Skidelsky, R. (1983), *John Maynard Keynes*, Vol. I *Hopes Betrayed 1883–1920*, London: Macmillan.
Somerville, H. (1931), 'Usury as a New Issue', *The Commonweal*, **XIV**, (2), Sept. 16.
Somerville, H. (1932), 'The Villain of the Economic Piece', *The Commonweal*, **XVII**, (3), Sept. 16.
Somerville, H. (1936), 'Mr Keynes and the Canonists,' *The Commonweal*, **XXIV**, (7), June 12.
Timlin, M.F. (1947), 'John Maynard Keynes', *Canadian Journal of Economics and Political Science*, **13**, (1), August.
Wattel, H.L. (ed.) (1985), *The Policy Consequences of John Maynard Keynes*, Armonk, New York: M.E. Sharpe.
Weiler, P. (1982), *The New Liberalism*, New York: Garland.
Winch, D. (1969), *Economics and Policy*, London: Hodder and Stoughton.

2 'A prodigy of constructive work': J. M. Keynes on *Indian Currency and Finance*

Robert W. Dimand

> Cecily, you will read your Political Economy in my absence. The chapter on the Fall of the Rupee you may omit. It is somewhat too sensational. Even these metallic problems have their melodramatic side.
>
> Miss Prism, in Oscar Wilde,
> *The Importance of Being Earnest.*

The great and lasting impact of *The Economic Consequences of the Peace* and *The General Theory of Employment, Interest and Money* has diverted attention from John Maynard Keynes's first professional success, *Indian Currency and Finance* (1913). By his thirtieth birthday, Keynes had advanced from a junior clerkship at the India Office to be a member of a Royal Commission on Indian Currency and Finance, editor of the *Economic Journal,* secretary of the Royal Economic Society, and invited guest lecturer at the London School of Economics, honours that were due to his writing on Indian finance. His Annexe to the Indian Currency Report was acclaimed by Alfred Marshall as 'a prodigy of constructive work. Verily we old men will have to hang ourselves, if young people can cut their way so straight and with such apparent ease through such great difficulties' (Pigou, 1925, p. 479). H. S. Foxwell's prediction in his 1913 review of Keynes's book that it was and 'is likely long to remain, the standard work on its subject' has been borne out, so that the *Economic Journal* review of the *Cambridge Economic History of India* observed that 'It is a pity to have to say on Chandravarkar's [sic] chapter on Money and Credit that those who wish to have a taste of the complexities of the Indian monetary system will still do better to read Keynes on *Indian Currency and Finance,* a work that he rightly admires' (Sayers, 1972, p. 593; Chaudhuri, 1984, p. 194).

Apart from its importance for the monetary history of India, *Indian Currency* is significant for the development of Keynes's views on monetary policy. It was written within the Cambridge monetary tradition of Marshall's testimony before the Gold and Silver Commission of 1887–88 and the Indian Currency Committee in 1899, which Keynes later edited in Marshall's *Official Papers* (1926). Even at such an early stage of his career, however, Keynes's proposal for a central bank and a managed currency rather than a return to the gold standard foreshadowed the advocacy of a managed currency in *A Tract on*

Monetary Reform (1923), his opposition to Britain's return to gold at the pre-war parity in 1925, and the celebrated 'Auri Sacra Fames' section in *A Treatise on Money* (1930) and *Essays in Persuasion* (1931) on the irrational importance given to gold. The gold exchange standard that Keynes expounded, and contrasted with a gold standard, in *Indian Currency* was a precursor of the Bretton Woods system.

Keynes entered the India Office in 1906, after finishing second out of 104 candidates on the Civil Service examination but far behind Otto Niemeyer who, after first inclining toward the India Office, took the only position open at the Treasury that year (Sayers, 1972, pp. 591–2; Keynes received 3498 marks out of 6000, Niemeyer 3917: JMK, XV, p.3). Keynes's early memoranda concerned the shipment of ten young Ayrshire bulls to Bombay and the dating of commissions of lieutenants, but he was soon transferred to the Revenue, Statistics and Commerce Department and entrusted, at the age of 24, with editing the India Office's annual report to Parliament. He resigned on his twenty-fifth birthday, 5 June 1908, to accept a lectureship at Cambridge but remained concerned with Indian topics. His first major article, 'Recent Economic Events in India', *Economic Journal,* March 1909 (JMK, XI) argued that the rise in Indian prices was due to a capital flow into India, rather than the reverse as had been assumed, and received a gratifying amount of attention for a first article: four Indian newspapers reviewed it, and it was read in proof by Lionel Abrahams, Financial Secretary for India and Keynes's mentor at the India Office, who wrote that 'I take the opportunity of thanking you for the assistance that I derived from the methods used in your paper in the *Economic Journal*' (JMK, XV, pp. 3, 11, 15–17, 38).

In the 1910–11 academic year, Keynes gave six lectures on 'Currency, Finance and the Level of Prices in India' at the London School of Economics and then at Cambridge. He drew on these lectures for a paper on 'Recent Developments of the Indian Currency Question', which was read to the quarterly meeting of the Royal Economic Society in March 1911 and then printed in Simla by the Government of India for private circulation among its officials, as well as being circulated by Abrahams at the India Office. This paper (JMK, XV, pp. 67–85) was the basis for *Indian Currency and Finance.*

India was on a monometallic silver standard from 1835 to 1893, when free coinage of silver was suspended after depreciation of the gold value of silver had reduced the sterling value of the Indian rupee. The depreciation had caused budgetary problems for the Government of India, whose 'home charges' such as pensions and interest on the public debt were denominated in sterling, which had a fixed gold value. Both the Herschell Committee of 1892 and the Fowler Committee of 1898–99 endorsed a gold standard for India, under which coined gold would circulate. Despite repeated statements by Government of India officials that a full gold standard was still the ultimate goal, noted Keynes, a gold-exchange standard had developed instead.

> The gold-exchange standard may be said to exist when gold does not circulate in a country to an appreciable extent, when the local currency is not necessarily redeemable in gold, but when the government or central bank makes arrangements for the provision of foreign remittances in gold at a fixed maximum rate in terms of the local currency (JMK, XV, p. 71).

In view of his later attitude towards classical economics, it is noteworthy that Keynes claimed classical antecedents for his favoured monetary standard:

> The gold-exchange standard, which resembles the currency proposed at the time of the bullionist controversy by Ricardo, who pointed out that a currency is in its most perfect state, when it consists of cheap metal, but of an equal value with the gold it professes to represent, arises out of the discovery that, so long as gold is available for payments of *international* indebtedness at an approximately constant rate in terms of the national currency, it is a matter of comparative indifference whether it actually *forms* the *national* currency; and that there is in fact an enormous saving of expense in using some cheaper material for the actual medium of exchange, India for example, having saved 20 millions in this way during the last ten years (JMK, XV, p. 70; cf. JMK, I, p. 22, emphasis in original).

Keynes noted that A. M. Lindsay, deputy secretary of the Bank of Bengal and one of the few advocates of a gold-exchange standard for India, entitled one of his pamphlets *Ricardo's Exchange Remedy* (JMK, I, p. 24). Ricardo's plan also reached the Indian Government through another Cambridge source – D. A. Barker, writing on *The Theory of Money* for the Cambridge Manuals of Science and Literature in 1913 while serving in the Indian Civil Service in Garhwal, discussed Ricardo's *Proposals for an Economic and Secure Currency* and its resemblance to Marshall's testimony to the Gold and Silver Commission (Barker, 1913, pp. 115–18).

Keynes also invoked the authority of John Stuart Mill for the belief that gold for international payments would come from bank reserves, rather than from internal circulation (JMK, I, p. 51; XV, p. 78), so that any gold circulated internally as coins was simply that much gold unavailable for external settlements.

Keynes established that the Indian monetary system was a gold-exchange standard, which had not been officially admitted, and urged movement away from, instead of continued change toward, a fully-fledged gold standard. British readers, accustomed to regarding Britain's gold standard as the ideal for which the rest of the world should strive, must have been startled to be told that a gold-exchange standard was 'the ideal currency of the future' (JMK, I, p. 25; XV, p. 69) and that India was 'in the forefront of monetary progress' (JMK, I, p. 182). The gold-exchange standard would provide as stable a value of money (even if in terms of only one commodity, gold) as the gold standard, while economizing on the holding of resources in the sterile form of gold by allowing for circulation of bank notes and token coinage and for holding international reserves in interest-bearing form.

Keynes noted that the Indian public's wasteful hoarding of gold had buffered the world economy against the inflationary effects of the Witwatersrand gold discoveries, 'Every one knows Jevons's description of India as the sink of the precious metals, always ready to absorb the redundant bullion of the West and to save Europe from the more violent disturbances to her price level'. He looked beyond even the gold-exchange standard to 'a more rational and stable basis' than gold for the standard of value: 'It is not likely that we shall leave permanently the most intimate adjustments of our economic organism at the mercy of a lucky prospector, a new chemical process, or a change of ideas in Asia' (JMK, I, pp. 70–71).

Keynes proposed that India's international reserves should be held increasingly in the form of liquid sterling assets rather than gold, and that accumulations in the hands of the Government of India in excess of the reserves needed to maintain a fixed exchange rate 'ought to be put at the disposal of the Indian money market and not converted into sterling'. The supply of credit money should be made elastic to accommodate the pronounced seasonal fluctuations in demand for money in India (JMK, I, pp. 126–7).

To provide a machinery for chanelling government funds into the Indian money market, providing an elastic currency, and ensuring the liquidity of the banking system, Keynes proposed the creation of a State Bank of India, absorbing the central bank functions then divided between the government and the three Presidency Banks of Bombay, Calcutta and Madras (JMK, I, pp. 166–8). A central bank was needed as lender of last resort and as guarantor of the liquidity of the Indian banking system because of the unsoundness of many Indian banks:

> One comic opera bank registered in Calcutta in 1910 put down [nominal] capital of £20,000,000, without having at the time of the last return any paid-up capital at all. Apart from this exceptional venture, the thirty-eight banks registered in 1910–11 had between them a nominal capital of £1,306,000 and a paid-up capital of £19,500. With enormous nominal capitals they combine high-sounding titles – the Bank of Asia, the East India Bank, the Hindustan Bank, the United Bank of Commerce, and so forth. Once established, their activities are not limited. One of these banks has included in its operations coach-building and medical attendance (JMK, I, pp. 162–3).

As Chandavarkar (1982, p. 780) notes, 'In 1913, on the very eve of these bank failures [of 55 Indian banks, 1913–14], Keynes had commented with almost prophetic insight on the vulnerability of Indian banks, due to their undercapitalization, inadequate cash reserves and speculative proclivities'.

In 1913 Keynes was offered the secretaryship of the newly-established Royal Commission on Indian Currency and Finance, a post which would normally have gone to a junior official of the India Office. Then, on the basis of proofs of *Indian Currency*, which were circulated at the India Office, Keynes was offered a seat on the commission rather than the secretaryship and so became, in Marshall's words of congratulation, 'the youngest member of the youngest Commission' (JMK, XV, p. 98). Keynes strongly influenced the Indian Currency Report, which rejected circulation of gold coin in favour of a gold exchange standard, and wrote, under his own signature, an Annexe to the Report proposing the establishment of a State Bank of India (JMK, XV, pp. 151–211). He served on the commission under the chairmanship of Austen Chamberlain, a former and future Chancellor of the Exchequer, and alongside Lord Kilbracken, who had been Keynes's superior at the India Office, and Sir Robert (later Lord) Chalmers, who was to be Keynes's wartime superior at the Treasury. Despite the eminence of colleagues, Keynes had great influence on the report because only he and Lionel Abrahams, one of the witnesses, had the necessary understanding of the workings of the Indian monetary system.

Keynes's acceptance, at the age of 30, as an authority on Indian finance is illustrated by the testimony of the secretary-treasurer of the Bank of Bengal, who was questioned about the flow of capital between India and England:

"It is all explained in Mr. Keynes's book." "What have you got to say to that?" he was asked. "I entirely agree with what Mr. Keynes says" (JMK, XV, p. 100).

Despite being ill with diphtheria in Mentone in the south of France in January 1914, and despite the wavering of some members of the Commission on the sections of the Report dealing with the reserves to be held by the Government of India (JMK, XV, pp. 220–67), Keynes managed to guide his fellow-commissioners to endorse a gold-exchange standard. Seignorage profits would be earned through issuing paper currency and token silver coinage for internal circulation. Official buying and selling of a gold-convertible currency, sterling, would keep the external value of the rupee constant without any need for costly shipment of gold bullion between India and England. The Government of India would gain from holding interest-bearing, liquid sterling assets in place of some of the gold in its external reserves. Abrahams was justified, however, in reproaching Keynes for failing to mention in his memorandum on the advantages of a central bank, that such profits from an economical currency could be used by the Indian Government for industrial investment, such as railway construction (JMK, XV, p. 214).

Although Professor J. S. Nicholson of Edinburgh University criticized the Indian Currency Report at length from the standpoint of the gold standard, the pressure of events rather than adverse comment shelved the report. During the First World War, the gold value of silver rose sufficiently to raise the intrinsic value of the metal content of the rupee above its face value, while the pound sterling ceased to be convertible into gold (see Keynes's testimony before the Indian Exchange and Currency Committee in 1919, JMK, XV, pp. 273–98). After 20 years of stability at an exchange rate of 1s 4d, the rupee rose to 2s 4d by December 1919 and then fell back to 1s in 1921. India did not get a central bank until 1935, when the Reserve Bank of India was created. The three Presidency Banks were amalgamated as the Imperial Bank of India in 1921, but this acted as a commercial bank rather than as a central monetary authority and, contrary to Keynes's desire for a seasonally elastic currency, raised its loan rates in the busy season (Chandavarkar, 1982, pp. 789-94).

Despite his lack of immediate influence on Indian monetary policy, Keynes's gold-exchange standard proposals in *Indian Currency and Finance* and the Annexe to the Indian Currency Report reappeared 30 years later in the Bretton Woods system, under which fixed exchange rates were maintained, not by gold flows, but by national central banks buying and selling a gold convertible reserve currency, the dollar.

Keynes's early writings on Indian finance were strongly embedded in the classical tradition of Ricardo, Mill and Marshall and did not share the major concern of Keynes's maturity, the determination of the level of output and employment. These writings do, however, display characteristic aspects of Keynes's later thought, notably his desire to devise a stable international monetary system that would be more flexible and less wasteful of resources than the gold standard and his emphasis on the crucial role of central banking in managing such a system. His work on this topic established him in both Whitehall and the academic community, at an early stage of his career, as a promising and significant authority on monetary questions at a time when his fellowship dissertation on probability and his Adam Smith Prize essay on index numbers were still unpublished.

References

Barker, D. A. (1913), *The Theory of Money*, The Cambridge Manuals of Science and Literature, Cambridge: Cambridge University Press.

Chandavarkar, A. G. (1982), 'Money and Credit, 1858–1947', in D. Kumar, with the assistance of M. Desai, (eds.), *The Cambridge Economic History of India*, Cambridge: Cambridge University Press, 762–803 .

Chaudhuri, P. (1984), review of *The Cambridge Economic History of India*, *Economic Journal*, **XCIV**, 192–4.

Foxwell, H . S. (1913), review of Keynes (1913), *Economic Journal*, **XXIII**, 561–72 .

Keynes, J. M. (1913), *Indian Currency and Finance*, London, Macmillan. [Reprinted as JMK, I, with altered pagination.]

Keynes, J. M. (1971–83), *The Collected Writings of John Maynard Keynes*, E. A. G. Robinson and D. E. Moggridge (eds.), Cambridge: Cambridge University Press for the Royal Economic Society, 29 vols [cited as JMK plus volume number].

Marshall, Alfred (1926), *Official Papers*, J. M. Keynes (ed.), London: Macmillan.

Nicholson, J. S. (1914), 'The Report on Indian Currency and Finance in Relation to the Gold Exchange Standard', *Economic Journal*, **XXIV**, 236–47.

Pigou, A. C. (ed.) (1925), *Memorials of Alfred Marshall,* London: Macmillan.
Sayers, R. S. (1972), 'The Young Keynes', *Economic Journal,* **LXXXII,** 591–9.

PART II

THE RECEPTION OF KEYNES'S *THE ECONOMIC CONSEQUENCES OF THE PEACE*

3 Something and nothing: the impact of J.M. Keynes's *The Economic Consequences of the Peace* in Britain, 1919–1921

John Hemery

The Economic Consequences of the Peace has been called 'one of the most influential books of the twentieth century' (Skidelsky, 1983, p. 384). Robert Skidelsky's admirable critique of the book and its reception in his recent biography of Keynes, *Hopes Betrayed,* illuminate the extent to which Keynes's work both embodied and generated a new perspective of the Versailles Treaty in particular and of international affairs in general (Skidelsky, 1983, pp. 376–402). Many assume that it was instrumental in the United States Senate's non-ratification of the Treaty, and in hardening the American government's attitude toward the repayment of Britain's war debt to the United States. In Germany it is reckoned to have strengthened resistance to the tentative *Erfullungspolitik* of early post-war German governments. In France it is said to have had the opposite effect of strengthening determination to enforce the terms of the Treaty. In Britain Keynes is widely credited with having amelio-rated the pip-squeezing spirit, so having enabled the government to change tack on the issue of reparations and open the way to a settlement.

While there is something in this general impression, it is not quite the whole picture. There is no doubt, however, that the book had a dramatic impact in Britain at the time of its publication. *The Economic Consequences of the Peace* (hereinafter, for the sake of brevity, *Economic Consequences*) was the subject of editorials and reviews in every newspaper and journal of substance, and in much of the pulp press. Almost immediately, Keynes's work somehow crystal-lized the issues which for so long had confounded the promised peace. As a popular newspaper, the *Star*, put it in February 1920, with the enviable economy of tabloid journalese, 'We are all Keynesites now' (Editorial, the *Star*, 13 Feb 1920).

An interesting question arises, though. To what extent was opinion *changed* by *Economic Consequences*? Despite the great clamour at the time, to what extent did the work fulfil Keynes's hope, expressed in his dedication of the book to 'the formation of the general opinion of the future', that he would help to bring about a change in the popular feeling towards Germany and the Treaty, which in turn would exert irresistible pressure for revision on the politicians?

A distinction in this respect must be made between the end product – that is, ultimate changes in policy on reparations and European recovery, and the relatively short term effects by which the impact of the book itself might be measured; in other words, before the publication of Keynes's subsequent works and before other events intervened to contribute to changes in political and public opinion.

In assessing the impact of the book on opinion in Britain, this chapter is divided into two parts. Keynes, of course, distinguished between two kinds of opinion: outside opinion, by which he meant the opinion of the public as expressed by the politicians and the newspapers, and inside opinion, being the views held by politicians, civil servants and others in government which they would not express openly (Keynes, 1922, p. 3). When Keynes's argument for the necessity of revising the Treaty burst upon the public imagination, the distance between the two opinions was indeed marked. Yet, as will be shown, the enthusiasm for Keynes's diagnoses and prescriptions even amongst outside opinion was by no means universal.

The impact on 'outside' opinion

In July 1919, when the Peace Treaty was presented to the House of Commons for ratification, only four MPs voted against it, and they did so only in protest at the denial of self-determination for Ireland.[1] Lloyd George's diplomacy was praised on all sides. But six months later, in December 1919 when Keynes's book was published, the public mood had already changed considerably. The prevailing feelings then were frustration and disillusionment; the war had been over for a year but peace and stability still seemed far off. The *Observer* noted, '1919 has been, in the main, a year of disappointment (for the Conference at Paris will not appear to history so different from the Congress of Vienna as we hoped it would), a year of unrest and misgiving, and dubious compromises and fallings from high ideals' (*Observer*, 21 December, 1919). A comic paper contained a cartoon of John Bull face to face with a menacing, haggard female, whose bonnet bore the inscription 'Peace'. 'Well!' said the representative of British life and character, 'You are not quite the Angel I imagined you this time last year!'[2] The public was ready for an explanation of why things hadn't turned out as promised, but from the Government there were only anodyne phrases and official secrecy. Into this collective sigh of frustrated hopes and deflated hatreds was lodged Keynes's quietly insistent prose. *Economic Consequences* provided not only an explanation for the Treaty's failure to bring peace, but also a set of concrete proposals for resolving the mess.

Outside opinion responded to Keynes's argument in three different ways. One group welcomed the book because it confirmed and articulated what they thought already – or at least felt subconsciously. *Economic Consequences*, and especially the portraits of the Big Four, showed the failed Peace to have been

the product not of wickedness but of weakness. Here was the last disillusionment, that the victory won at such cost had been fumbled and fudged by
incompetent diplomacy. Thus revision of the Treaty's inequities perhaps at last
would yield the elusive settled peace. Skidelsky notes, '[*Economic Consequences*] captured a mood. It said with great authority, flashing advocacy and
moral indignation what "educated" opinion wanted said' (Skidelsky, 1983, p.
399).

It is difficult to put a figure on the proportion of public opinion who reacted
in this way, but it was a significant minority view, perhaps even a silent
majority view. It included most members of the Free Liberal and Labour Parties
and, broadly speaking, the liberal intelligentsia. The *Nation* observed, 'The book
is a thunderbolt ... the first heavy shot that has been fired in the war which the
intellectuals opened on the statesmen the moment they realised what a piece of
work the Treaty was' (*Nation*, 13 December, 1919). The *Daily News* endorsed
Keynes's analysis: 'No-one who follows it will lightly dispute his conclusions.... The burden of the present volume is the future, the dominating need
to salve what can still be salved, instead of watching the wreck break up
altogether'(*Daily News*, 23 December, 1919). The *Star* noted similarly,
'Keynes exhibits the political stupidity of [the Peace] Terms with crushing
completeness.... [*Economic Consequences*] is a strong courageous book, in-
controvertible in logic and humane in spirit' (*Star*, 23 December, 1919). R.W.
Seton Watson, writing in *The New Europe*, referred to both Keynes's book and
the sensation it had caused as 'signs of a return to sanity' (*New Europe*, 1
January, 1920).

Thus with *Economic Consequences* Keynes touched an immediately responsive chord in a large part of outside opinion. Many, such as C.F.G.
Masterman (syndicated in the northern provincial press), criticized the politicians or the process of secret diplomacy for what was frequently termed the
betrayal of victory and of the sacrifice of those who had died.[3] H. N. Brailsford
wrote in the *Labour Leader*, 'If grass grows on the quays of Hamburg, and
thistles seed on the boulevards of Vienna, it will be because the Supreme Four
dictated a peace of strangulation' (*Labour Leader*, 1 January, 1920).

Almost all of Keynes's initial reviewers recognized the power of the book.
The *Manchester Guardian* noted, 'If many economists had his wit, his elo-
quence, his easy address in stating confused and intricate problems, their
science would never have been called dismal' (*Manchester Guardian*, 24
December, 1919). The economists themselves offered Keynes enthusiastic
support. A.C. Pigou called the book 'absolutely splendid and quite unanswer-
able'.[4] R.G. Hawtrey was 'full of admiration'.[5] C.R. Way wrote, 'My congratulations if you are still out of gaol, my condolences if you are bombed on
the way to the station'.[6]

For some in this first group of outside opinion, of all parties or none, *Economic Consequences* reawakened their compassion, or their rationality towards the treatment of Germany; it provided the final antidote to the drug of wartime hatred and propaganda. Mrs V.R. Drummond Fraser wrote to Keynes from Manchester University,

> We all feel that you have given a real impetus towards right....Incidentally, I may add, I – having given my two sons – 'was' among those who were short-sighted enough to wish to ruin Germany's future, without thought of our own and of all our dear ones gave their fine, young lives for.[7]

Not all were so readily conquered. A second group of outside opinion rejected Keynes's argument precisely *because* Keynes asked them to put aside sweet revenge in favour of something as viscerally unsatisfying as enlightened self-interest. This was the group – also a minority but a vocal one – of irreconcilables, the jingoistic nationalists who were not at all interested in 'letting the Germans off'. For many in Britain who had palpably lost everything else in the war, it remained important at least to punish the bastards who had caused all the misery. The right wing *Sunday Chronicle* typified this reaction when it called the Treaty 'a sentence on Germany's crime', and attacked Keynes for 'staying on [at Paris] till the last possible moment and then resigning' (*Sunday Chronicle*, 21 December, 1919).

The third and perhaps most substantial response to Keynes's work by outside opinion acknowledged the strength of his argument, and conceded that in an ideal world his economic and financial proposals probably would work. But they criticized either his premises or his political naïveté. Henry Wickham Steed, in his celebrated three-column blast in *The Times*, dismissed *Economic Consequences* as 'the cry of an academic mind,... "political economy" in revolt against the facts and forces of actual political existence'. Wickham Steed concluded, 'If the war taught one lesson above all others it was that the calculations of economists, bankers and financial experts, who preached the impossibility of war because "it would not pay", were perilous nonsense' (*The Times*, 5 January, 1920). The *Times Literary Supplement* noted, 'The ultimate criticism of Mr Keynes' book will be this, that it is the criticism of a man who is occupied with and interested only in one part of the [Treaty]. For the political side he appears to have little interest or understanding'(*The Times Literary Supplement*, 15 January, 1920). The *Spectator* observed that Keynes's proposal for a European Free Trade Union was perhaps premature, at a time when economic barricades were going up all over the continent. The *Spectator* concluded, '...the world is not governed by economical forces alone, and we do not blame the statesmen at Paris for declining to be guided by Mr Keynes if he gave them such political advice as he sets forth in this book'(*Spectator*, 20 December, 1919).

This was the point on which outside and inside opinion in Britain converged. Though most recognized the imperfections of the Treaty, most clung to the view rejected by Keynes that security issues had to take precedence. 'Nothing could be more fatal', noted the *Observer*, 'than to rebuild [German] economic strength ... without any new political security whatever for Europe'(*Observer*, 4 January, 1920). At Paris, concessions had had to be made to the Utopian vision of Wilson's League, and the Covenant had been swallowed with more or less good grace, if with tongue in cheek. But precisely because the European statesmen were being set to the pursuit of the Holy Grail, they took care to shore up the homestead against the chance that its divine mysteries might not protect them. To Keynes's charge that the economic aspects of the Treaty were unwise or unworkable, the politicians could reply that the obstinately enduring realities of power could not be ignored, whether at the Peace Conference or after.

The intensity of the debate between these competing outside views was good for sales. 8000 copies of *Economic Consequences* were sold in Britain at a price of 8s.6d in the first six weeks after publication.[8] Another 10 000 had been sold barely two months later. The figures might have been higher. 2000 copies were lost at sea in transit from the printers.[9] Keynes complained, 'I fear that I have lost a considerable volume of sale by reason of the fact that the booksellers have never been able to get enough copies to expose the book for sale over the counter, and have only been able to fulfil orders placed in advance'.[10] After the initial surge of demand, with sales of over a thousand copies a week, the book continued to sell steadily during the ensuing months at the rate of a few hundred a week. In all, 24 000 copies of *Economic Consequences* were sold in Britain in the first year of publication.[11] Keynes was referred to at the time as 'a soft-faced man who has done exceedingly well out of the Peace'.

The full price of 8s.6d, though not expensive by the standards of the day, still made the purchase of *Economic Consequences* a burden for most working people. Keynes received many requests for a cheaper edition. K. E. Royds, Secretary of the Women's International League, wrote that a cheap edition would ensure its worldwide circulation and help to make it the nucleus of a Revisionist campaign.[12] Herbert Peet of the Society of Friends offered to distribute a cheap edition through the Workers Educational Association and the Adult Schools.[13] Keynes sought estimates from Macmillans for printings of ten or twenty thousand copies to be sold at 1s. or 2s.6d. Harold Storey of the Labour Party's Publications Department urged Keynes to go for the lower figure: 'The difference between the two prices', he argued, 'would be the difference between a very good circulation and a great popular campaign'.[14] Keynes opted, nevertheless, for the higher price. The cheap edition was published in March 1920, and was distributed by the Labour Research Department at 2s.6d in a limited special offer (one copy free with every dozen ordered) to trade unions, co-operative societies, and Labour Party bodies. 1s.10d per copy went to Keynes. All 10 000 copies printed were sold by September 1920.[15] In proportion to normal sales of academic and popular books in the period, *Economic Consequences* sold well. In comparison, 10 000 copies of Norman Angell's *The Great Illusion* were sold within three years of its publication. Yet in the context of influence upon public opinion it may be noted that the readership of these seminal works was insignificant in relation, for example, to the 55 000 daily circulation even of one popular newspaper, the *Morning Post*.[16]

In the course of the two years after the publication of *Economic Consequences* the particular views held by outside opinion in Britain did not change much. When Keynes's sequel to *Economic Consequences*, *A Revision of the Treaty*, came out in the midst of the economic slump in January 1922, the papers which had supported him in 1919 still supported him, with the added piquancy that he (and they) had been proved to have been right all along about the need for revision. And the papers which had castigated him in 1919 rebuked him again for his pro-Germanism or for his tone of moral superiority. *The Times* revived its earlier criticism of Keynes's fondness for the enemy, noting,

> In this pretty interpretation of recent history there is no suggestion that Germany may be in any sense to blame, that intentional German obstruction may be one of the chief causes of our present plight. Mr Keynes ... welcomes every indication that [German] evasion has been successful, that her stubbornness and importunity are weakening the firm front of the Allies (*The Times*, 10 January, 1922).

The *Spectator* complained, 'Mr Keynes, with his taunting superiority ...does not write like a good Englishman ... he ought to write with the English ethos, with a real indignation against German materialism and the Doctrine of Might run mad' (*Spectator*, 14 January, 1922). The *Morning Post* observed, with undimmed wartime spirit,

> ... the British public has never approached the problem of Reparations from an economic point of view. We doubt if they have ever expected to get much tangible reparation from Germany, but they have always insisted *on moral grounds* that Germany should be compelled to pay to the uttermost farthing. Mr Keynes, luminous, learned, and logical, fails to take into his calculations the moral issues at all... The German rulers launched the war and waged it in brutal fashion, and did so with the whole-hearted support of the German people. Having failed they must pay the penalty (*Morning Post*, 10 January, 1922, emphasis in original).

Apart from these reflex responses, almost all the reviews of Keynes's *A Revision of the Treaty* recognized that economic forces could no longer simply be subordinated to political desires. The journal *Imperial Commerce* noted, 'We are all wiser now on Reparations. Trade is bad. Something must be blamed and by a fortuitousness as remarkable as it is happy, the right thing is at last hit upon' (*Imperial Commerce*, February, 1922). The *Manchester Guardian* observed,

'... a few optimists still dream of a couple of thousand millions. But already the dismal suspicion has spread that if they were paid they would plunge us into years of capriciously distributed unemployment... Why not cut our losses under the Versailles Treaty without waiting for them to grow?' (*Manchester Guardian*, 15 October, 1921).

The *Economist* on the other hand remained cautious. While acknowledging the validity of Keynes's economic analysis, it lamented,

> Frankly, we despair of being able to write off the slate the history of the last three years and reopen this question *de novo*.... To challenge the whole basis of the Treaty of Versailles, though it might be in the ultimate interests of humanity, would postpone the question indefinitely during the present generation (*Economist*, 11 February, 1922).

Instead, the *Economist* recognized the only sensible solution, 'the radical modification of the impossible payments demanded from Germany by means of negotiation'.

The new element in the public responses to Keynes's second book thus was the much broader acceptance that the reparations regime was impracticable and would have somehow to be changed. In the midst of depression and unemployment in Britain at the end of 1921, Keynes's diagnoses and prescriptions carried considerably more weight with outside opinion than they had done at the height of the post-war boom.

The impact on 'inside' opinion
Inside opinion in Britain, especially the views on reparation and European recovery of those politicians and civil servants who were the source of Government policy at the time, remained essentially unchanged by *Economic Consequences*. As the decision-makers and Keynes knew, the substantive obstacles to the Peace he sought lay not in London, but largely in Berlin, Paris and Washington. Just as with outside opinion, though, there were those who favoured Keynes's arguments and those who were opposed.

Strongly in his favour were his former colleagues at the Treasury, and especially those in the Treasury's international 'A' Division who had worked with Keynes in December 1918 in assessing Germany's capacity to pay reparations and on the general problems of European economic recovery. S.D. Waley of 'A' Division wrote to Keynes, 'If I am made Archbishop of Canterbury...I shall order a chapter to be read from the pulpit every Sunday'.[17] Waley's colleague George Peel, who had been a member of Keynes's staff in the Treasury delegation at Paris, exulted similarly that Keynes had shown '... the path of possible reconciliation and of true statesmanship, that higher statesmanship which touches hands with humanity'.[18] The Treasury's Permanent Secretary, Warren Fisher, told Keynes that he had read *Economic*

Consequences 'with great gladness', and concluded, 'My prayer is that many, in all parts, will read the book'.[19]

As well as support from the Treasury, Keynes had private messages of praise and congratulations from many members of the Government, though none supported him in public.[20] Only Andrew Bonar Law, Keynes's wartime Chancellor at the Treasury and Lloyd George's partner in coalition, demurred. He wrote to Keynes, 'I do not agree altogether with your point of view and in spite of your logic you will not find that things turn out in accordance with your theorems...'.[21] From the Prime Minister there was no response. Though Keynes sent presentation copies to virtually all his former associates in government, he did not send one to Lloyd George with whom he had worked closely in Paris. Keynes heard, though, that 'while parts of [the book] made him wild, on the whole he liked it, "for it showed he was a cleverer man than Wilson" which after all is the thing that matters!'[22]

Yet for all the deluge of praise from the Insiders on the brilliance and courage of the book, there was serious criticism too. It took three forms. Some felt that Keynes had betrayed his trust as a servant of the Crown. In an age not attuned to official indiscretion, Keynes's resort to publicity was regarded by his detractors as dishonourable. This, together with his resignation from his duties at the Peace Conference, undermined for them the credibility of his work.[23]

The second and more substantial inside criticism was that, in going public, Keynes had damaged relations with those, especially in the United States and France, whose support for moderation of the Treaty terms was considered essential. Lord Reading, lately British ambassador in Washington, was reported to be 'in despair because of the harm it would do in America'.[24] The Foreign Secretary, Lord Curzon, called *Economic Consequences* 'wonderful Republican propaganda' and doubted that Wilson would ever recover from it.[25] Sir Hardman Lever, head of the Treasury's wartime mission in the United States, lamented

> I am in very close agreement with you, particularly in your appreciation of the European position, but I cannot help regretting your animadversions on our friend the President. They may be entirely justified, but the American people are apt to be susceptible in these matters, and I fear your book will not help forward the Anglo-American rapprochement, which to my mind is the most immediately important international movement.[26]

The Chancellor of the Exchequer, Austen Chamberlain, while agreeing broadly with Keynes's analysis and privately having 'chortled with joy' over the Conference chapter, noted nevertheless,

> ...I am sorry that you should impute bad faith to all the Allied negotiators. The position is difficult enough, the need for some world agreement as to a solution is urgent enough, and I think your argument would have been more persuasive and

compelling if you could have found it in your heart to base your case entirely on the economic facts and to omit the moral denunciations.[27]

Keynes disagreed. He replied to Chamberlain,

> As regards the effect on the Americans, I should be very sorry if I were to make a difficult position worse. But in this realm who can predict the final reaction of his words. The policy of humbugging with the Americans has been given a pretty good trial and has not proved a brilliant success. Who can say but that the candid expression of views sincerely held may not open their eyes in the long run more effectively than oceans of semi-sincere platform sentiment?[28]

R.H. Brand, personal adviser to Lord Robert Cecil when Cecil headed the Supreme Economic Council at Paris, and Keynes's closest collaborator at the Peace Conference in his attempts at moderating the reparations clauses of the Treaty, observed, 'Notwithstanding its power I regret the inclusion of your chapter on the Conference, because I think it may impair your usefulness in helping in the near future.... I am very sorry for this outcome.'[29] Brand's fears for the practical damage that the book might do to Keynes's influence were borne out soon after. He and Keynes were among the prime movers with a group of Neutral bankers promoting a major international loan for European recovery.[30] They planned to secure the support of as many prominent financiers and politicians as possible before launching the scheme through the auspices of the League of Nations, and with maximum public pressure so to induce individual national governments to participate in the loan. Once *Economic Consequences* had been published, however, no British Government Minister and few supporters of the Lloyd George Coalition would put their names to a scheme associated with Keynes lest they be thought to be tacitly endorsing Keynes's attack on the Government's conduct of the peace negotiations.[31] In the end Keynes was obliged to remove his own name from the list of supporters of the international loan scheme of which he was the author in order to avoid jeopardising the chances of its adoption in the capitals so recently bludgeoned in his book.[32]

The third major inside criticism of *Economic Consequences* was perhaps the most telling: it referred to the value of the Peace Treaty as a whole, and the damage done to it by Keynes's call for revision. This was the view strongly held by the Foreign Office, who argued not that the Treaty was perfect but that it was essential for restoring Europe to peace, and the adjustment of its more obviously unworkable provisions could be arranged subsequently. Any encouragement of early revision would, in this view, only invite a torrent of irredentism and undo the painful diplomatic work of the previous twelve months.

James Headlam-Morley of the Political Intelligence Department at the

Foreign Office warned that revision of the Treaty might cause,

> ...not only the overthrow of the present government, but also most probably a
> rupture of the alliance with France and a complete unsettlement of the whole of
> Europe; it might give the Germans the opportunity, while Great Britain was
> seriously compromised in Asia, to destroy all that has been done and to plunge the
> whole affairs of the world into confusion.[33]

The object of Allied policy, he argued, ought to be '...to impose upon
[Germany] conditions which would so limit her power as to prevent her
becoming in the future what she had shown herself in the past, a danger to the
independence of the neighbouring states'.[34]

Headlam-Morley's senior, Sir Eyre Crowe, concurred. He urged that
Headlam-Morley should undertake a general defence of the Treaty:

> A great deal of harm has undoubtedly been done by the indiscriminate and one-
> sided onslaught of Mr Keynes, especially in America, where Mr Keynes' book is
> the principal armoury for an organised campaign against this country. A book by
> Headlam-Morley – not in appearance for official publication – would constitute a
> most effective and at the same time sober antidote. It would do good both in America
> and in France.[35]

In the course of the ensuing two months Headlam-Morley wrote a detailed and
devastating riposte to *Economic Consequences.*[36] But the Foreign Office backed
away from the confrontation. The Foreign Secretary, Lord Curzon, endorsed
Headlam-Morley's argument but deprecated publication in any way associat-
ing the work with the Foreign Office because of the power of Headlam-
Morley's criticism of Keynes. Crowe minuted, 'Is it desirable, is it even quite
proper, that Keynes should be so attacked, or exposed, by the Foreign Office?...
Only the Prime Minister could decide this....'[37] The official counter-argument
to *Economic Consequences* thus went by default. Ultimately, in August 1920,
Lloyd George did give Headlam-Morley permission to publish his work under
a pseudonym in periodicals, but by that time events had moved on and the issue,
for media purposes, was dead. Headlam-Morley found no daily or Sunday
newspaper which would accept his articles, and the only authoritative inside
defence of the Treaty and of its negotiation was never published.[38]

  In this period, however, the Foreign Office was not the arbiter of British
foreign policy; the Prime Minister was. The ultimate test of the impact of
Economic Consequences in Britain thus is the extent to which Lloyd George's
policy may have been modified either by Keynes's argument, or by the pressure
of the electorate's response to it. In neither respect can a change be observed.
From a time well before the Armistice it had been Lloyd George's intention to
impose upon Germany as large an indemnity as possible, limited only by her
capacity to pay.[39] He had specifically excepted reparations when accepting the

Fourteen Points as the basis for peace negotiations.[40] Just as Keynes did, Lloyd George wanted a fixed sum representing Germany's total obligation. But the French, and Lloyd George's own principal advisers on indemnity (Lords Sumner and Cunliffe and the Prime Minister of Australia, William Hughes) argued that the only figure acceptable was the aggregate of Allied damage claims, whatever that might amount to. Because French claims naturally were so much greater than those of Britain, and because Lloyd George suspected that the French probably would inflate them further, he refused to settle on any fixed sum until a firm deal had been struck on what he regarded as fair proportions in which German payments would be divided amongst the Allies. Twice at the Peace Conference he was offered a quarter share, but held out for not less than a third.[41] Lloyd George was determined to secure a settlement which fulfilled his three minimum criteria: punishing the Germans, placating his own electorate and, crucially, preventing the French from getting away with the loot.

At Paris, Lloyd George confidently expected that his aim would be achieved within twelve months. He conceded that the popular feeling of the moment stood in the way of fixing a sum just then at any figure acceptable to either French or British public opinion, hence he adopted the convenient temporary expedient of the Reparation Commission. But he also fastened on Keynes's suggestion – the last advice Keynes offered before resigning – that Germany should be given the opportunity, after the Treaty had been signed and passions had cooled, of putting forward her own offer of a lump sum in full settlement of her obligation to make reparation. Lloyd George succeeded in convincing his colleagues on the Council of Four to incorporate this crucial modification in a Protocol to the Treaty. Lloyd George was confident that in her own interests Germany would make a sensible offer, and that the Allies, in their own interests, would accept it.

Within six months, though, much had changed, undermining the basis of Lloyd George's strategy. President Wilson had suffered his stroke, the United States government was in paralysis, and American participation either in enforcing the Treaty or in assisting European recovery looked increasingly in doubt. In the absence of the Americans, the French looked to enforcing reparations as an alternative form of security against German resurgence, and were moulding the Reparation Commission to their purpose. In addition, the British budget was still heavily in deficit, with the American debt looming large. Lloyd George did not need Keynes to remind him that fixing the reparations bill and starting German payments was essential. He told a Cabinet conference at Downing Street on the day Keynes's book was published, 'we could not ever expect to get the whole indemnity, but the Germans for a certain number of years would pay something'.[42] Consequently, he settled forthwith the proportions issue with the French,[43] and successfully promoted the extension of the time laid down by Protocol to the Treaty within which Germany could offer a lump sum settlement.

As from the Peace Conference onwards, therefore, the British continued their private but persistent efforts to induce the German government to propose and the French government to accept a workable reparations settlement based upon a fixed sum distributed amongst the Allies in agreed proportions. As Headlam-Morley argued, the British were already pursuing the revision which Keynes so persuasively demanded, but in a rather quieter fashion. He observed pointedly,

> On the whole in these matters the tradition of the British Government is the right one. When a thing has been done, you accept it as finished, you do not trouble yourself much about historical arguments and personal criticisms, but, accepting the facts, pass on to the next matters which have to be dealt with. If a mistake has been made, you shrug your shoulders, you recognise it in private conversation, you say little about it in public, but quietly do what you can to remedy it. [44]

It is to be remembered as well that as early as April 1919, Lloyd George had accepted Keynes's comprehensive Scheme for the Rehabilitation of European Credit which lay at the heart of his remedies in *Economic Consequences*. It had been commended to the Prime Minister by the Chancellor, Austen Chamberlain, as being marked by all Keynes's 'fertility of resource'. That was true enough; Keynes's fertile mind had been put to concealing the essential point that most of the resources were to come from the Americans. Lloyd George had submitted the Scheme to his colleagues on the Council of Four as the policy of the British government but the Americans had seen through the wrapping to the present within and the package was rejected. So Lloyd George soldiered on from Conference to inconclusive Conference in 1920 and 1921 in pursuit of the formula which somehow would resolve the international political dilemmas impeding a settlement. At every stage, though, he wanted a solution which could be achieved within the Treaty. He was unmoved by Keynes's call for revision, or by the widespread popular support which Keynes's views increasingly enjoyed.

The fact that Keynes's indiscretion in publishing *Economic Consequences* was regretted, and that his remedies for Europe were not adopted, in no way implies that he had entirely lost the confidence of the British government. On the contrary, even at the height of the controversy over *Economic Consequences,* his advice continued to be sought by the Treasury, the Foreign Office and the British Delegation to the Reparations Commission on issues of domestic and foreign finance, and on points of interpretation of the Treaty terms. Keynes, after all, with his American colleague Thomas Lamont, had drafted the Reparations Chapter whose provisions he came only months later to vilify; hence he was well-placed to explain the intentions of the peacemak-ers.[45]

Keynes remained on close terms with his wartime colleague Basil Blackett, who from 1919 to 1922 was head of the Finance Division in the Treasury responsible for British domestic and foreign financial policy. Blackett repeat-edly urged on the Government the unilateral cancellation of Allied war debts to Britain, and later a moratorium on German reparations payments, as the means of breaking the logjam in reparations diplomacy and clearing the way for a comprehensive settlement such as Keynes proposed.[46] In the end, having had no success, Blackett sent his rejected Cabinet memoranda to Keynes, asking him to have them published anonymously so that at least the weight of his argument might bear upon outside opinion, as *Economic Consequences* had done. The reasons for Blackett's failure are the same reasons for which Keynes's arguments were ignored. In part, it was because the perceived political imperatives of the moment, both domestic and foreign, still exerted a more powerful hold over Lloyd George and his colleagues than did financial or economic considerations no matter how serious. As Sir Ernest Cassel noted at the time, 'The politicians ruling the world don't pay the least attention to the advice of the economists'.[47]

Ironically, however, there was one final and decisive source of inside opposition to Keynes's ideas which was not political but economic. Keynes's prescriptions for European recovery were rejected by the British government because they conflicted with British post-war economic policy. The Govern-ment identified credit inflation as the main obstacle to the restoration of Britain's economic and financial position in the world. To counter it they kept interest rates high, progressively retired government debt and pursued bal-anced budgets.[48] This painful adherence to deflation at home thus was at odds with Keynes's remedies for Europe, at least in so far as those remedies had to be financed by Britain through the cancellation of debts owed to her, or by the further extension and guarantee of sterling credits abroad. The British Treasury were certain that they could not finance European reconstruction by them-selves, and there was very little sign of other governments offering any large scale assistance. Hence, even though the British government largely agreed with Keynes's view of the economic consequences of the Peace, there were compelling reasons of *domestic* economic orthodoxy for avoiding the *foreign* economic policies he recommended.

Conclusion

If it is the case, then, that inside opinion in Britain was essentially unaffected by *Economic Consequences*, how is the impact of the book to be measured? Some advance in outside opinion perhaps may be inferred from Parliamentary debates before and after publication. In February 1920, two months after

Economic Consequences came out, 60 MPs voted for revision of the Treaty, an improvement of 56 since the ratification debate seven months earlier. Keynes's arguments were acknowledged on both sides of the House, especially in respect of the impracticability of fulfilment by the enemy of many of the Peace terms, and the damage being done by them to the economic life of Europe. Nevertheless, four times as many MPs still opposed revision as supported it.[49]

Keynes may more safely be argued to have prepared the political ground for adjustments in policy towards Germany and Europe subsequently made necessary by the pressure of events. Keynes's work, for all the hostility to its hauteur and inverted morality, provided the British government with an effectively unchallenged rationale for the modification of the reparations regime, as well as with an electorate whose views had been given form by Keynes, or who had become inured in the course of the long debate over *Economic Consequences* to the loss of their illusions. In 1921, as Britain's economy slumped, and as Keynes's predictions of the economic consequences of the Peace were daily more evidently borne out in Britain, so all but the most reluctant became reconciled to his arguments, and the way was open for economic wisdom and political wisdom for once to coincide.

Overall, Keynes's *Economic Consequences of the Peace* paradoxically may have had a surprisingly limited impact in Britain. It enjoyed, of course, immense literary success, and brought both Keynes and economics from the academic margins to the forefront of public and political consciousness. That in itself might be said to be enough of an achievement. Some advance in outside opinion may properly be attributed solely to Keynes's book. But the decisive swing on the part of those who opposed his views came when Keynes's arguments no longer had to be taken simply on faith, but could be seen to be working in practice. As for inside opinion, the measurable impact of the book on policy was effectively nil, at least in the short term. Keynes, on the other hand, continued to be consulted by those in Government on questions of economic and financial policy, hence perhaps he might be said to have unified inside and outside opinion in himself.

Notes

1.   Hansard, 5th Series, HC 1919, vol 118, 21 July, 1919; Treaty of Peace Bill: Ayes 163, Noes 4.
2.   Cited in *Daily Telegraph*, 26 November, 1919.
3.   C. F. G. Masterman, *Northern Echo*, 27 December, 1919; *Birmingham Gazette*, 27 December, 1919; *York Gazette*, 10 January, 1920. Masterman observed, 'Politicians did their best to lose the peace'.
4.   Pigou to Keynes, (n.d.), Papers of J. M. Keynes, EC 1/1. I am indebted to Judith Allen and the Marshall Library of Economics, Cambridge, and especially to Dr Michael Halls and the Fellows of King's College, Cambridge for having allowed me to consult the Keynes Papers in the preparation of this chapter while the Papers were closed for cataloguing.
5.   Hawtrey to Keynes, 18 December, 1919 JMK, EC 1/1.
6.   Way to Keynes, 22 December, 1919 EC 1/1.

7. Mrs V. R. Drummond Fraser to Keynes, 21 January, 1920, JMK, EC l/20.
8. Daniel Macmillan to Keynes, 21 January, 1920, JMK, EC 1/4.
9. Many of these copies were washed ashore in Denmark, dried out and sold. This says much for the entrepreneurial spirit of the Danish beachcombing community and for the efficiency of their tumble driers, as well as for the power of Keynes's ideas.
10. Keynes to A. Harcourt (New York), 29 January, 1920, JMK, EC 1/4.
11. 17 173 copies were sold in the first fifteen weeks to 1 April 1920. Monthly sales thereafter: April 2433; May 1159; June 769; July 797; August 450; then an average of 100 per week to the end of October 1920. A reprint of 2500 was then ordered, of which only a third had been sold by 1 June 1921. Sales averaged 18 copies a week for the twelve weeks 1 March to 2 June 1921 (JMK, EC 1/4).
12. Royds to Keynes, 16 January, 1920, JMK, EC 1/3.
13. Peet to Keynes, 19 January, 1920, JMK, EC1/3.
14. Storey to Keynes, 9 February, 1920, JMK, EC 1/3.
15. G. D. H. Cole, Honorary Secretary, Labour Research Department, to Keynes, 11 November, 1920, JMK, EC 1/3.
16. I am indebted to my colleague at the University of Leeds, Dr Keith Wilson, for these comparative data.
17. S. D. Waley to Keynes, 19 December, 1919, JMK, EC 1/1.
18. Peel to Keynes, 18 December, 1919, JMK, EC 1/1.
19. N. F. W. Fisher to Keynes, 17 December, 1919, JMK, EC 1/1.
20. Lord Beaverbrook (20.12.19), Lord Curzon (23.12.19), E. F. Wise (23.12.19), J. F. Williams (1.1.20), A. Steel-Maitland (4.1.20), E. S. Montagu (6.1.20), Lord Bryce (n.d.) to Keynes, JMK, EC 1/2.
21. A. Bonar Law to Keynes, 30 December, 1919, JMK, EC 1/1
22. Josiah Stamp to Keynes, 8 February, 1920, quoting J. C. C. Davidson, then Private Secretary to the Chancellor of the Exchequer, Austen Chamberlain, JMK, EC 1/2.
23. For an expression of this view see the *Spectator*, 20 December, 1919. A number of the early reviews of *Economic Consequences* drew the parallel between Keynes's work and the Bullitt revelations in the United States. See also especially Austen Chamberlain to Keynes, 22 December, 1919, JMK, EC 1/1.
24. R. McKenna to Keynes, 27 December, 1919, JMK, EC 1/1.
25. Curzon to Keynes, 23 December, 1919, JMK, EC 1/2.
26. Lever to Keynes, 16 December, 1919, JMK, EC 1/1.
27. Chamberlain to Keynes, 22 December, 1919, JMK, EC 1/1.
28. Keynes to Chamberlain, 28 December, 1919, JMK, EC 1/1.
29. Brand to Keynes, 27 December, 1919, JMK, EC 1/1. Brand had urged Keynes before publication to tone down his criticisms. Brand to Keynes, 7 November, 1919, JMK, EC 1/1.
30. The Amsterdam Memorial, written by Keynes and published in the major Allied and neutral capitals on 15 January, 1920. Memoranda and correspondence in JMK, FI/1.
31. Notable amongst these was Lord Reading, who withdrew his support following the publication of *Economic Consequences*. Similarly Sir Brien Cokayne, Governor of the Bank of England, Sir Robert Chalmers, former Joint Permanent Secretary to the Treasury, and Lord Northcliffe withheld their signatures. Brand to Keynes, 23 January, 1920, JMK, FI /1.
32. Lord Robert Cecil to Keynes, 31 December, 1919 and 6 January, 1920, JMK, FI /1. Cecil observed that Keynes's signature 'might antagonise powerful influences' both in Britain and in the United States. Cecil added, 'Perhaps you are a little hard on Wilson. He was very badly treated by us who ought to have supported and helped him with that information and experience which he and his advisors so sadly lacked'.
33. Memorandum by J. W. Headlam-Morley, 12 March, 1920, FO 371/4267/7067/185791, Public Record Office, Kew (hereinafter FO 371).
34. Ibid.
35. E. A. Crowe minute, 27 March, 1920, FO 371/4267/7067/185791.
36. Memorandum by J. W. Headlam-Morley, 8 June, 1920, FO 371/4270/7067/202471.

37. E. A. Crowe minute, 16 June, 1920, FO 371/4270/7067/202471.
38. Headlam-Morley minute, 13 August, 1920, FO 371/4270/7067/202471; text of Headlam-Morley's articles, Folios 97-191; (also in the Headlam-Morley Papers, Churchill College Archive, Cambridge).
39. For a detailed examination of Lloyd George's policy and diplomacy at the Peace Conference and after, see Hemery (forthcoming).
40. WC 497, 5.11.18, CAB 23/8, PRO. On 3 November 1918, at the pre-Armistice negotiations, Lloyd George declared that he thought it would be a mistake to put into the Armistice Terms anything that would lead the Germans to suppose that the Allies wanted a war indemnity. He added, 'When you get the Armistice and the bridgeheads on the Rhine, you can interpret this as you like' (Burnett, 1940, vol I, p 403). See also Lentin, 1985.
41. Council of Four, 14 March, 1919, and meeting of Informal Reparations Committee, 26 March, 1919, PRO FO 608/292, T1/12407/48046; JMK, PT/l and PT/2.
42. Notes of a conference at Downing Street, 12 December, 1919, PRO T194/4.
43. Avenol–Blackett Agreement, 13 December, 1919, PRO T194/4.
44. J. W. Headlam-Morley memorandum, 8 June, 1920, (Introduction, p. 4), FO 371/4270/7067/202471.
45. On resigning his post at Paris after the Treaty had been presented to the Germans, Keynes wrote to Chamberlain, 'I must have my hands quite free' (Keynes to Chamberlain, 21 May, 1919, JMK, PT/1). His early departure from the scene of the crime allowed them at least to be fairly well washed.
46. Blackett memoranda: 'Inter-Allied and Anglo-American Debts' (CP 584), 2.2.20, CAB 24/102; 'German Reparations: The Need for a Readjustment of the Present Schedule of Payments' (CP 3527) and 'Reparation in Kind' (CP 3528), 16 November, 1921, FO 371/6038/2740J18/22283; 'Cancellation of Inter-Allied Debt', 14 December, 1921, PRO T194/8.
47. Cassel to R. H. Brand, 5 May, 1921, Brand Papers, Bodleian Library, Box 37.
48. Minutes and Memoranda, Interim and Final Reports of the Treasury Committee on Currency and Exchanges after the War, 15 August, 1918 and 3 December, 1919, PRO T1/12434/53026 and T1/12437/53595. Austin Harrison referred to the prevailing belief that money would emanate from some 'Aladdin's cave of credit-issue' (*The English Review*, December 1921) .
49. Hansard, 5th Series, HC 1920, vol 125, 12 February, 1920, Debate on the Address, Amendment for Revision of the Treaty. Ayes 60, Noes 254.

References

Burnett, P.M. (1940), *Reparation at the Paris Peace Conference*, New York: Columbia University Press.

Hemery, J.A. (forthcoming), *Money and Power*, Cambridge: Cambridge University Press.

Keynes, J.M. (1919), *The Economic Consequences of the Peace* reprinted in *The Collected Writings of John Maynard Keynes*, Vol II (1977), London: Macmillan.

Keynes, J.M. (1922), *A Revision of the Treaty*, reprinted in the *Collected Writings of John Maynard Keynes*, Vol. III (1971), London: Macmillan.

Keynes, J.M. (n.d.), Papers of J.M. Keynes, EC1/, (unpublished), Modern Archive, King's College Library, Cambridge.

Lentin, A. (1985), *Lloyd George, Woodrow Wilson and the Guilt of Germany*, Baton Rouge, Louisiana: Louisiana State University Press.

Skidelsky, R. (1983), *John Maynard Keynes: Hopes Betrayed 1883–1920*, London: Macmillan.

4 American responses to Keynes's *The Economic Consequences of the Peace*

Charles P. Blitch

The American edition of *The Economic Consequences of the Peace* was published in January 1920. Keynes, who was having difficulty finding an American publisher, gave an advance copy of the English edition to Felix Frankfurter who was passing through London on the way home from the Paris Peace Conference. He had been a legal adviser to the United States delegation and had become friendly with Keynes. Frankfurter read the book on the ship to New York and recommended it to Walter Lippmann who was a reader for the newly established publishing firm of Harcourt, Brace and Howe. This firm subsequently contracted for the American rights (Harrod, p. 290). Arrangements were made for advance publication of three excerpts from the book in the liberal magazine, *The New Republic*. The first excerpt was the chapter containing the devastating character sketch of President Woodrow Wilson which may have had a negative influence on liberal opinion regarding the Treaty of Versailles (JMK, XVII, 42). The book was a phenomenal success for a non-fiction volume with the first edition of 20 000 copies selling out immediately. By the end of April 1920, some 70 000 copies had been sold in the United States (Skidelsky, p. 394).

For a better understanding of the reaction in America to Keynes's book, a summary of the political situation in the United States at the time of its publication is necessary. President Wilson presented the Treaty of Versailles with its League of Nations Covenant to the Senate for ratification upon his return from Paris in July 1919. The Senate was composed of 47 Democrats and 49 Republicans. Lacking even in a simple majority, Wilson's party was far short of the two-thirds vote required for approval of the treaty. Opponents of the treaty were divided into two groups, one led by Senator Henry Cabot Lodge, chairman of the Senate Foreign Relations Committee, who proposed amendments to the League Covenant; and the isolationists headed by Senator William E. Borah, who opposed the treaty in any form. Lodge delayed the Senate vote on the treaty by holding extensive public hearings before the Foreign Relations Committee which lasted almost two months. In September 1919, President Wilson undertook a tour of the nation to arouse public support for the treaty in general and for the League of Nations Covenant in particular. Wilson's health gave way and he collapsed before the tour ended and suffered a stroke in early October. The Senate's first vote on the treaty came on 19 November 1919, and it was twice rejected – both with and without the reservations proposed by Lodge – though the opposition failed to command the two-thirds vote which would have defeated the treaty definitively. During January and February widespread public pressure was put on the Senate for quick ratification (Bailey, pp. 53–104; 187–92). Since the English edition of *The Economic Consequences of the Peace* was not published until December 1919, it had no influence on this first round of Senate voting. In response to public opinion the Senate voted on 9 February 1920 to reconsider the treaty (Bailey, p. 254). Thus the publication of Keynes's book in America coincided with the public and Senate debate over the reconsideration of the Treaty of Versailles.

Keynes's savage indictment of the Treaty of Versailles as a Carthaginian peace, his contention that the terms of the treaty were set secretly by the Council of Four, and in particular his unflattering portrait of President Woodrow Wilson as a Presbyterian elder 'bamboozled' by the clever Lloyd George and the sharp-witted Clemenceau dismayed and disturbed former members of the American contingent at Paris. Their reactions to these charges were expressed in letters to the editors of major newspapers, speeches and reviews of the book.

One of the earliest responses came from David Hunter Miller who had been the chief legal adviser to the American Commission to Negotiate Peace. He wrote an article for the *New York Evening Post* of 6 February 1920, in which he accused Keynes of completely misinterpreting the reparations section of the treaty by writing, 'Until the treaty is altered, therefore, Germany has in effect engaged herself to hand over to the Allies the whole of her surplus production in perpetuity'. This resulted in an exchange of letters between Keynes and Miller, published in the *Post*, with neither antagonist changing positions (JMK, XVII, pp. 32–7). In a letter to *The Times* of London on 16 February 1920, John Foster Dulles, a legal and financial consultant to the Americans at Paris, concluded:

> If every ambiguity in the pre-Armistice conditions is to be resolved in favour of Germany; if every ambiguity in the treaty is to be resolved in a sense oppressive to Germany; if it be assumed that the Reparations Commission is to exercise its function in a spirit obviously destructive of the interests of the Allies and of the economic re-establishment of Europe; then Mr. Keynes's condemnation of the treaty is explicable. If, however, the immense practical difficulties with which the Peace Conference had to deal in a brief period of time are taken into account; if the broad constructive purpose of the treaty is borne in mind, and its provisions (already elastic) are liberally construed and applied; and if a Reparations Commission is created which will, as intended, exercise its powers with wisdom and in accordance with the true interests of the nations which it represents; then the treaty can be regarded as a statesman-like accomplishment. I myself adopt the latter hypothesis (JMK, XVII, pp. 24–6).

Professor Clive Day of Yale University, who served as a specialist on the Balkans at Paris, reviewed the book for the *American Economic Review*. Day contended the book should be treated as a political tract rather than as a contribution to economic literature as its tone was 'theatrical' and the account of many points of fact were 'distorted and misleading' (Barber, p. 198).

The closest counterpart to Keynes on the American Commission was Professor Allyn A. Young, an economist on leave from Cornell University, who served as chief of the Economics and Statistics Division of the US technical staff. As such he was intimately involved in the economic settlements of the treaty. Young was the American representative to and chairman of the subcommission on commercial treaties; he was an alternate for the US members on the Economic Commission; and he was economic adviser to the American delegates on the Reparations Commission. Diaries kept by several persons in the American group all refer to Young's informal consultations regarding reparations, commercial treaties, labour problems and other matters of an economic nature. Young and Keynes met in Paris and briefly discussed the German indemnities, but they did not form a close relationship. Nevertheless, Keynes had a presentation copy of his book sent to Young by his American publisher.

The divergent perspectives of Young and Keynes on the Treaty
Allyn Young returned from Paris in May 1919, and in an interview with a reporter gave his opinion of the Treaty of Versailles and League of Nations:

> There is no question that the peace treaty as finally drafted accords more severe treatment to the Germans than they would have received under a rigid interpretation of the Fourteen Points. The treaty is in many respects a compromise between the French demand that France receive a position of absolute guaranteed safety for a long term of years and the Fourteen Points. The concessions made by France are, however, much larger than those made by the United States delegation.
>
> The principal concession to the British is the inclusion of war pensions in the list of claims upon which the indemnity to be paid by Germany is based. It is not to be expected that Germany will be able to pay enough to cover all the just claims against her for damages to persons and property, plus the cost of military pensions but the inclusion of military pensions in the list of claims for which Germany is to assume liability gives England a larger proportion of the total German payments than she would otherwise have had. The concessions made to Japan in the Shantung Peninsula were indefensible, being nothing more than a price paid for Japan's adherence to the League of Nations.
>
> It is not true that President Wilson went to Paris without a plan for a League. It is probable that his plan was not worked out in detail, but the broad outlines were in his mind. President Wilson's original plan was in some respects very close to the plan developed by General Smuts. The present Covenant is a combination of the British and American views, modified at some points to meet the objections raised by France and the smaller states.

Most critics of the League make the mistake of expecting that its machinery would be automatic, that it would provide a perfect mechanism for preventing war and adjusting international disputes. These critics miss the fundamental purpose underlying the League proposal to assure an open and frank discussion of international difficulties by reasonable representatives of the different nations.

The purpose of the League is to make international misunderstandings more difficult and less frequent. What particular sort of League we get is not nearly so important as that we should get some kind of League.

It would be a great misfortune if the treaty were not ratified by the Senate, because while it is a compromise, it is the best treaty that can be obtained at the present time (*New York Times*, 31 May 1919, 20: 1).

Upon receipt of the presentation copy of *The Economic Consequences of the Peace*, Young wrote Keynes saying, 'I am very glad to have the copy of your book. It is a magnificent and courageous achievement. It makes me regret, more than ever, that I did not see more of you at Paris...On almost every point of fact and policy I agree with you' (AAY to JMK, 11 February 1920). Where Young did not agree with the author was on the matter of President Wilson's part in the making of the treaty. He wrote:

Most of all I feel you concede too little to the President. He held the cards, and might have conceivably have dictated the peace. But what would have come of it?...He was beaten, not by the sophistries of Lloyd George, or the immovability of Clemenceau, but by the sheer force of circumstances. The peace of Versailles was a democratic peace in the sense that it was a fair expression of prevailing sentiment in the victorious democracies. It was an inevitable precipitation of the slow poisons with which human souls have been drugged during the war. Perhaps the people would have responded differently to a different type of leadership, but that had nothing to do with the situation as it was.

The President held all the cards, but the cards had little value. He did not have back of his program the solid sanction of public opinion in France or England, or even in the United States, – and Clemenceau knew it. At a Council of Vienna he could have pulled it off; at Paris he had to reckon with democracy: that is with domestic politics. His failure was inevitable. I do not believe that anyone in his place could have succeeded (AAY to JMK, 11 February, 1920).

Keynes, in his reply, thanked Young for his comments and made the following reference to the President's role:

As regards my picture of the President, you must remember two things: one, that I wrote it in July immediately after I left Paris and before I had any knowledge of his illness, and, two, that although it is generally taken as an attack on him, I intended it not so much as an attack as an explanation. Many persons here believe that in spite of appearances the Treaty must be in accordance with our engagements because the President had acquiesed in it. I thought it necessary therefore to give a human explanation of how it came about that this is not so. In spite of everything I say about him, and all my disappointments, I still believe that essentially the President played a nobler part at Paris than any of his colleagues (JMK to AAY, 28 February 1920).

Young reviewed the book for *The New Republic* (Young, 1919–20, pp. 388–9) and, although agreeing with Keynes on most of his facts and figures and saying that he had put his finger upon the gravest defects of the treaty, he stressed the point that the treaty was framed in terms of the political situation of the time. He wrote, 'What this scene lacks is background. Mr. Keynes knows the things that should be in that background, but he tucks them away into a dim corner and forgets them. That, I imagine, is because the background is political, and Mr. Keynes is impatient of political considerations. He thinks in terms of economic right and economic wrong and personal responsibility'. And as he had in his letter to Keynes, he defended the President:

> It was not the adroitness of Lloyd George or the laconic single-mindedness of Clemenceau that balked the President. It was what he could see over their shoulders. Nothing less than unified and courageous leadership could have lifted public opinion in the Allied countries (including the United States) up to the level of a peace that would have been an honest fulfillment of pre-armistice pledges. Public opinion – still reacting to war stimuli – was always there, in the meeting room of the Council of Four, in the guise of 'the domestic political situation'. It was Clemenceau's strength and Wilson's weakness (Young, 1919–20, **21**, pp. 388–9).

On the matter of German reparations, Young agreed with Keynes on his estimate of Germany's capacity to pay – ten billion dollars. Against Keynes's charge that Germany was forced to sign a 'blank check' which could be used to strangle its economic recovery, Young argued that the Reparations Commission would, as the passions of war diminished, use its powers wisely because forcing Germany to pay unreasonable amounts would endanger the whole economic structure of Europe. Young said that the main value of Keynes's book was in the development 'of a more intelligent and more liberal public opinion'. In concluding his review, he wrote, 'As against Mr. Keynes's brilliancy, insight and courage, there must be put certain elements of strain, of exaggeration, of effort for dramatic consistency. But for all that his book is nothing so much as a fresh breeze coming into a plain where poisonous gases are yet hanging' (Young, *The New Republic*, **21**, p. 389).

In private correspondence with Professor F. W. Taussig of Harvard University, who had sent Young a proof of his review for the *Quarterly Journal of Economics*, Young was still more direct, 'I am sorry Keynes has lessened the generally wholesome effect of his book by exaggeration and by what you properly term "utopianism". The book seems to have been written in a white heat and contains things which Keynes himself, in later years, will regret' (AAY to FWT, 25 February 1920).

The Young–Keynes public controversy
At a luncheon meeting of the League of Free Nations (whose goal was US membership in the League of Nations) on 27 March 1920, Young and two other

former members of the American peace commission took part in a panel discussion of *The Economic Consequences of the Peace*. The moderator was Alvin Johnson, editor of *The New Republic*, and the other panelists were Paul Cravath, former financial adviser, and David Hunter Miller. Cravath was sympathetic to Keynes's proposal that the treaty be revised, arguing that the economic sections of the treaty did not comply with Wilson's Fourteen Points and that unless these economic terms were changed nothing could stop Europe from falling into chaos. Miller once again attacked Keynes's views on reparations and prophesied that when the treaty was examined in the light of history, it would be found that the peace was a peace of equity and fairness and the nearest approach to justice ever reached by humanity. He asserted that 'Keynes's book would substitute reaction for progress, injustice for justice and tyranny for freedom'.

In his remarks Young said nothing was further from the fact, as asserted by Keynes, that the treaty was made in secret by four statesmen. With reference to Keynes's account of President Wilson's role in making the treaty, Young read extracts from Keynes's letter of 28 February saying his characterization of the President was done to convince the English public that the treaty was wrong, but that he personally regarded the President as the noblest figure at Paris. No newspaper reporters were present and Young was unaware that a stenographer recorded the discussion for printing for members of the sponsoring organization. An account of the meeting was published in a major New York city newspaper the next day with a summary of Young's comments as well as those of the others (*New York Times*, 28 March 1920, 1: 8). Although no further reports appeared in the New York city press during the month of April, several state newspapers reported Young's remarks, and some made editorial comments, mostly unfavourable, on Keynes's tactics. In early May Walter Lippmann, an editor at *The New Republic*, wrote Young about the situation:

> A great deal of discussion seems to have been aroused by the letter from Keynes to you which has now gotten into print. I would be grateful to you if you could send me a copy of whatever you have given out for publication. It raises a rather serious moral question about Keynes and I want to be in possession of all the facts in case we have to comment upon the matter (WL to AAY, 4 May 1920).

Young replied that he had never released Keynes's letter for publication and that he had quoted one sentence, rather inaccurately, at the talk in New York. He sent Lippmann a copy of the pertinent paragraph from the letter (AAY to WL, 6 May 1920). Lippmann's answer characterized the general tenor of the discussion about Keynes's letter:

> I am very glad to have your letter of May 6 with the paragraph from Keynes. I am afraid that a totally false impression of what you did say and what Keynes said has

gotten abroad. People are saying that Keynes wrote you that his whole characteri-
sation of the President was made to produce a definite effect, in other words as
propaganda, and that it did not represent his sincere conviction about the President
(WL to AAY, 7 May 1920).

Keynes, who subscribed to an American newspaper clipping service, wrote
Young that he had received a number of cuttings from newspapers which were
highly critical, and enclosed an editorial from a Syracuse paper. (The copy of
the editorial that Young received did not identify the name of the paper or the
date of publication.) He gently chastised Young for quoting from private
correspondence without permission and for not quoting verbatim. He suggested
that the two letters between himself and Young be published to clarify the
situation. He also enclosed a proposed public statement to be issued by his
American publisher along with the letters.

The editorial which Keynes enclosed condemned him for being the worst
kind of hypocritical propagandist:

Confession an Offense

Professor John Maynard Keynes, an English economist and author of 'The Economic Consequences of the Peace', abused President Wilson shamefully in his
book, picturing him in the last conference of the 'Big Four' in the role of an ignorant,
stupid, old Presbyterian elder who proved an easy victim of the two alert confidence
men of remarkable power and understanding in the arts and wiles of European
statesmanship. He says Wilson's 'moral collapse' at Paris was one of the world's
greatest tragedies.

But he didn't mean what he said, this fellow, according to a letter recently
received from him by Professor A. A. Young of Cornell University, who quotes
Keynes as disclaiming any other purpose in his gross portrayal than to arouse a
demand in the English mind in favour of having the Versailles treaty modified.
'Otherwise my argument would not have been convincing to the English public', it
is said Keynes wrote, adding: 'Of course, I recognised President Wilson was the
noblest figure at Paris'.

History in time will inscribe with pretty fair accuracy the work Woodrow Wilson
performed in Paris and measure out the merit of reward in public approbation he or
his memory is entitled to, but if the Young advices are beyond question, no history
could record a worst exhibition of extreme bad taste, a more cold-blooded violation
of a public trust, than that of an English propagandist operating under the guise of
an economist.

The proposed public statement which Keynes enclosed for Young's information
read as follows:

My attention has been called in a mail just arrived from the United States to a speech
made by Professor Allyn Young at a luncheon held under the auspices of the League
of Free Nations Association on March 27 for the discussion of my book, 'The
Economic Consequences of the Peace'. In this speech Professor Young referred,
without permission and not verbatim, to private correspondence. These references of

his have been, through no intention on his part, the subject of widespread misrepresentation in the American press. I am stated in some quarters to have admitted in a letter to Professor Young that I gave a misleading impression of President Wilson in order to serve propaganda purposes in England. There is not a word of truth in this. The point of my letter to Professor Young was, first, that if I were writing now I should lay greater stress, in explaining the President's action, on impending illness (of which I was then unaware): and second, that my account of the President was not dragged in but was a necessary part of my purpose in order to explain how so apparently upright a man came to accept a Peace contrary to our engagements.

But I should like to take this opportunity of pointing out that while I blamed the President for deceiving himself, and for being imperfectly equipped for his task, I also represented him as being influenced by fine motives and as the champion, in intention, of ideal causes. Human beings, however, so much prefer to be thought wicked than stupid, that this account of mine is considered to be a violent attack, as compared with my treatment of those to whom I ascribe more wits and less idealism.

The actual text of my correspondence with Professor Young is given below.

Young answered that he agreed to the publication of the two letters but requested omission of part of his letter which violated confidences of the Peace Conference. He apologized by writing, 'My reference to your letter in my talk at New York was made on the spur of the moment and was an indiscretion which I regret'. He then explained his real concern about Keynes's portrayal of President Wilson:

> What I have regretted is that your book has been used in this country as a weapon against the President by men who are really very much further removed from your position than they are from the President's. There is no large and effective body of liberal opinion here, so far as the Treaty and international relations in general are concerned, except that which supports the President. The President stands for the best we have and men like myself find our only possible course of action in supporting him. Just now there is only the choice between his policies, on the one hand, and provincial isolation and selfishness on the other. Your book was written, first of all, of course, for an English audience. I am very sure that you yourself, if you had been writing primarily for American readers, would have said in your book something very much like what you said in your letter to me. The practical effect of anything that weakens the prestige of the President just now is to strengthen reaction....
>
> This long explanation is merely for the purpose of making clear my own attitude with respect to your book. On the facts in the case you are fundamentally right; and yet our own situation is such that a man who agrees with you is bound to count himself among the supporters of the President. I referred to your letter without the slightest intention of reflecting on your own attitude, but merely by way of giving a supplementary explanation that might in some measure be of service to the President (AAY to JMK, 10 June 1920).

Young wrote further that the whole matter had died down in the United States and it probably would not be worthwhile to Keynes to revive it. He pointed out that major metropolitan papers and weeklies had not taken it up. He left the decision to Keynes (AAY to JMK, 10 June 1920).

Evidently Young's reply mollified Keynes. In a letter to Young in late June, he wrote that in view of what Young said, and the fact that a long time had passed, he would take no further steps about the publication of the correspondence and had cabled his publisher accordingly (JMK to AAY, 29 June 1920).

Allyn Young's final assessment of Keynes's book came indirectly in a presentation prepared for a lecture series under the auspices of the *Philadelphia Public Ledger* given by former members of the American delegation at Paris. The series, titled 'What Really Happened at Paris', was organized for presentation at the Philadelphia Academy of Music beginning on 10 December 1920. Young's talk was about the economic aspects of the treaty. Clearly referring to Keynes's view of the economic settlements, he said:

> I have also emphasised ... the element of compromise, concession, mutual give-and-take, in the economic clauses. Just here is where the critics of those clauses find their opportunity. The critic is prone to think in terms of clear-cut principles of absolute right and wrong. Compromise is a departure from principle. It is easy, then, to find serious flaws in these economic clauses, reached as they were through compromise and agreement. You may believe that Germany should have been more severely dealt with, or you may believe, as I do, that the economic clauses, as a whole, are unwisely harsh and exacting. In either case the clauses depart from your standards of what they ought to be.
>
> But not one of the critics, so far as I know, has ever dealt with the matter with complete candor. Not one of them has squarely faced the alternatives. What would they have had the President do, when he saw that although the great and essential interests of the peace could be safeguarded, there were a good many important points in the economic settlement upon which agreement could be had only through concession? Would they have had the American representatives abandon the Conference and return to the United States? Or would they have had the President and his associates dictate the economic terms and force them down the throats of our Allies? The two alternatives are equally unthinkable. Left to themselves, with the firm, persistent, steadying pressure from America withdrawn, the various conflicting forces at Paris, if perchance they could have been brought into any sort of agreement, could have produced a treaty that would have delivered the world over to militarism, imperialism, and economic suicide. On the other hand, peace terms dictated to the Allies might have been signed but would not have been accepted. Either course would have meant prolonged bitterness and misunderstanding, new dissensions in Europe, the overturning of governments, and a clear field for militarism – or worse.
>
> Look the facts squarely in the face, and there is no other conclusion than that the only way out and the only way forward was and is through international agreement and understanding. And as things were – and remain – agreement and understanding among the Allies were – and are – the indispensable prerequisites to any larger and more inclusive agreements. There is no other road to the maintaining of peace or mending of the wrecked economic structure of Europe. A refusal to see in the situation any questions save those of absolute economic right or wrong is not far removed from sheer intolerance (Young, 1921, pp. 294–5).

Young once again defended President Wilson saying, '...those who were associated with the President in Paris will tell you how supremely quick and alert he was in discussion or conference, and how easily and accurately he penetrated to the heart of the most complicated proposal' (Young, 1921, p. 296). Young gave his overall view of the treaty and its economic clauses:

> It is a hard and exacting document – it could and should have been nothing else – and makes some regrettable but necessary concessions to the prevailing state of mind in Europe, and especially to the political exigencies of the situation...Many of the economic clauses of the treaty are parts of a temporary scaffolding set up to hold things in place until a more enduring structure can be erected. The treaty does not propose to settle the economic relations in the European states for all time. It is a forward-looking document. It leaves the way open for new and, it is to be hoped, better adjustments just as soon as the political situation in Europe makes these settlements possible. In the long run the economic settlement will be just what the world makes of it (Young, 1921, p. 304).

The whole series was published in the Philadelphia paper and also in major foreign newspapers, and later in book form.

There is no doubt that Keynes read Young's lecture for there is a tart reference to it in his book, *A Revision of the Treaty*. Referring to his first book on the treaty, Keynes wrote that most insiders accepted his main conclusions about the treaty, and appended the following footnote: ' "Its merely colourable fulfilment of solemn contracts with a defeated nation, its timorous failure to reckon with economic realities", as Professor Allyn Young wrote in a review of my book. Yet Professor Young has thought right, nevertheless, to make himself a partial apologist of the Treaty, and to describe it as "a forward-looking document"' (JMK, III, 2n). In a final letter to Keynes on the subject, Young expressed this sentiment:

> The difference between your position and mine is obvious. In England the practical problem was merely the revision of a Treaty which had already been accepted. Here the issue was whether the Treaty should be accepted or rejected. I believed, and still believe, that America should have accepted the Treaty and then should have done all that it could to secure its revision. We rejected on unworthy grounds, not on your grounds. Support of the Treaty means one thing in England, another thing in the United States (AAY to JMK, 7 February 1922).

The book and Treaty ratification

The United States Senate had reconsidered the Treaty of Versailles, and on 19 March 1920 failed to ratify the Treaty with the amendments by the required two-thirds majority vote although it received a simple majority approval (Bailey, pp. 266–7). As Keynes's tome was published in America in mid-January, shortly before the Senate voted to reconsider the treaty, the question of its influence on the Senate vote is worth asking.

Two of Keynes's biographers deny that *The Economic Consequences of the Peace* had any significant effect on the Senate's rejection of the treaty. Harrod argued that although the book was used by political opponents of the President, the treaty was already doomed by the controversy surrounding the League of Nations Covenant (Harrod, p. 293). Skidelsky, while acknowledging it as a very influential book, is of the opinion that President Wilson himself caused the defeat of the treaty by refusing to accept any amendments. He does conclude that Keynes's picture of the President being 'bamboozled' by the wily European leaders strengthened isolationist sentiment in the United States (Skidelsky, p. 398).

Historian Thomas A. Bailey, who chronicled the details of the Senate ratification fight, has argued that Keynes's book contributed significantly to the rejection of the treaty by causing liberals and liberal journals to turn against the President. He cited the cases of *The New Republic* and *The Nation* as examples of the liberal press which took editorial stands against ratification. Bailey maintained that Keynes's book 'undoubtedly had a powerful effect in stirring up opposition both within and without the halls of Congress' (Bailey, p. 23).

The strongest claim that *The Economic Consequences of the Peace* caused the United States to abandon the Treaty of Versailles has come from the pen of Etienne Mantoux, son of Paul Mantoux, the translator at private meetings of the Council of Four. Mantoux noted that Senator William E. Borah, the leading isolationist and bitter opponent of the Treaty and League of Nations, read long passages from the book on the Senate floor the day the debate on reconsideration of the Treaty began. Borah, who held a copy of the book aloft and recited Keynes's credentials said, 'His contention is that the German Treaty consigns continental Europe to perpetual famine and chronic revolution; that unless the Treaty is completely revised and rewritten, it must inevitably result that the economic system of Europe will be destroyed' (*Congressional Record,* Vol. 59, p. 2696). After reading extracts from the chapter asserting that President Wilson was tricked by Lloyd George and Clemenceau, Borah concluded his remarks as follows:

> I have no doubt that my colleagues and many other people have thought that I have been a little severe in my language toward the men who represented France and England at the conference, but nothing I can say within the parliamentary rules of this Chamber would be too severe. When you think of the fact that they have lightly wrecked the entire economic system of an entire continent and reduced to starvation millions of people and perhaps prevented world peace from coming at this decade, there is no language too severe for such men. I am not passing judgment upon them: I am reading the judgment of a man who sat there, an educated gentlemen, an instructed gentlemen, advising against this and denouncing those who finally consummated it. This Treaty in its consequences is a crime born of blind revenge and insatiable greed (*Congressional Record*, Vol. 59, p. 697).

Mantoux further invoked General Jan Smuts, leader of the South African delegation at Paris, in support of his position. Smuts, referring to Keynes's book, asserted: 'It helped finish Wilson, and it strengthened the Americans against the League' (Mantoux, p. 10). Mantoux concluded:

> Judging from the use of Mr. Keynes's book during the debate over the Peace Treaty, it is hard to find fault with General Smut's comments. The book was seized by the President's opponents as a first-rate weapon in the fight then raging. It was quoted extensively as evidence of the infamous deeds committed at Paris, in which America would not connive (Mantoux, p. 10).

As the Senate vote on the treaty with the Lodge reservations failed by only seven votes to receive a two-thirds majority, it is tempting to speculate that Keynes's volume was a critical factor in the defeat. But Wilson's tactics must also bear some responsibility for the outcome. The President refused to accept any compromise and ordered the Democrats in the Senate to vote against the Lodge version. Even so, 21 Democrats voted with the majority while only 23 remained loyal to Wilson. Ironically, the Wilson loyalists joined the die-hard isolationists to reject the Treaty of Versailles with its League of Nations Covenant (Bailey, pp. 266–7).

Conclusion

J. M. Keynes's *The Economic Consequences of the Peace* had an important and influential impact on American perception of the Treaty of Versailles and its League Covenant. For the enemies of the treaty and the League, it became a major weapon in the fight against Senate ratification. It was quoted widely in and out of Congress as evidence of the misdeeds done at Paris by crafty European statesmen who had successfully misled the President. For the friends of the treaty it furnished information about the economic plight of Europe which made it even more necessary for the United States to join the League of Nations and to be represented on the Reparations Commission in order to make the peace wise, just and lasting (Skidelsky, p. 399). The major reason why the Treaty of Versailles was not ratified appears to be the fact that the United States was not ready to assume a position of world leadership. Acceptance of the treaty meant joining the League of Nations and playing a major role in European and world affairs. This neither the Senate nor the country was prepared to do.

This whole episode, however, had some further ramifications. Keynes's polemical skills, as manifested in *The Economic Consequences of the Peace*, brought him notoriety in the United States. But those same skills produced some hard feelings among some leading American economists who – on points of analysis – should have been Keynes's natural allies.

References

Bailey, T.A. (1947), *Woodrow Wilson and the Great Betrayal*, New York: Macmillan.
Barber, W.J. (1984), *From New Era to New Deal*, Cambridge: Cambridge University Press.
Congressional Record, (1920), **59**, Part III, (Washington, DC: US Printing Office.
Harrod, R.F. (1951), *The Life of John Maynard Keynes*, London: Macmillan.
Johnson, E. (ed.), (1977), 'Activities 1920–1922', *The Collected Writings of John Maynard Keynes*, Vol. XVIII, London: Macmillan.
Keynes, J.M. (1919), *The Economic Consequences of the Peace*, reprinted in *The Collected Writings of John Maynard Keynes* in Vol II, (1977), London: Macmillan.
Keynes, J.M. (1971), 'A Revision of the Treaty', *The Collected Writings of John Maynard Keynes*, Vol. III, London: Macmillan.
Mantoux, E. (1952), *The Carthaginian Peace or the Economic Consequences of Mr. Keynes*, New York: Scribner's.
New York Times, 31 May 1919, 20: 8; 28 March 1920, II, 1: 8.
Skidelsky, R. (1983), *John Maynard Keynes: Hopes Betrayed 1883–1920*, London: Macmillan.
Young, A.A. (1921), 'The Economic Settlement', in E. M. House and C. Seymour (eds), *What Really Happened at Paris*, New York: Scribner's.
Young, A.A. (1919–1920), 'The Economics of the Treaty', *The New Republic*, 21 pp. 388–9 .
Young, A.A. (1920–23), Correspondence, (unpublished manuscripts), Manuscripts, Widener Library Archives, Harvard University, Folders J–L, S–W.

5 The impact of Keynes's *The Economic Consequences of the Peace* in Italy, 1919–1921

Domenico da Empoli

While on holiday in Rome in April 1920, John Maynard Keynes wrote as follows to Norman Davis (who had served as the chief American adviser to the Reparation Commission at the Paris Peace Conference), 'In Rome I find that my views are adopted *universally* and the contentions of my book are accepted by all Italian parties virtually without exception' (JMK, Vol. xvii, p. 40, emphasis in the original).[1]

Although the first part of Keynes's statement was undoubtedly true, this chapter intends to show that the reasons for the 'universal adoption' of *The Economic Consequences of the Peace* (hereafter referred to as *ECP*) arose primarily from the negative attitude of Italians toward the Paris Peace Conference, rather than from a careful analysis and evaluation of the book's contentions.

I

The principal concern of the Italian delegation at the Paris Conference centred on claims for neighbouring territories, formerly under Austrian rule, whose inhabitants were mostly Italian. Public opinion in Italy was highly sensitive on this subject, especially with regard to the fate of the town of Fiume whose National Council had requested incorporation into Italy on 30 October 1918. (Fiume, however, had not been included in the prospective Italian war claims set out in the London Agreement of 26 April 1915.)

Throughout the entire war, Italy's main adversary had been the Austro-Hungarian Empire on which Italy had declared war with the opening of hostilities on 24 May 1915. The declaration of war on Germany came more than a year later – on 25 August 1916. The damages imposed on Italy by the German army were considerably smaller than those produced by the Austro-Hungarian army. This may explain, at least in part, why the problem of reparations from Germany – which was central to the argument of *ECP* – was not considered by the Italian public to be of the utmost significance. The peace treaty with Austria, signed in Saint Germain-en-Laye on 10 September 1919, was more important for Italians than the treaty signed in Versailles.

Italians were nevertheless very critical of the Conference in Paris because their territorial aspirations on the Eastern frontier had been frustrated. Keynes's criticism, though directed at a different issue, was regarded by Italian public opinion as another demonstration of the unsoundness of the procedures and outcomes of the Conference. This accounted for the popularity of *ECP* in Italy. Despite their commendatory tone, very few of the Italian commentaries on Keynes's work contained a thorough appreciation of the book's central thesis.

In order to set out clearly the Italian attitude toward the Paris Conference, it is worthwhile recalling that Italian claims had received quite a cold reception from Lloyd George and Clemenceau and had been treated with open hostility by President Wilson. Wilson's principles set him against any 'imperialist' territorial expansion and he favoured the consolidation of the young Jugoslav state. He also believed that his position was shared by most Italians and that their government did not truly represent popular opinion. At a crucial point in the negotiations, Wilson registered his fundamental disagreement with Prime Minister Orlando's request for Italian control of Fiume. He did so in a direct appeal to the Italian public, published in newspapers on 23 April 1919, arguing that it was in Italy's best interest to follow his advice rather than that of their own Prime Minister.

Wilson's appeal (quite unprecedented in the relationships between allied governments) took Orlando by surprise. The Italian Prime Minister was unable to find a better solution than to leave Paris for Rome where he won approval for his negotiating position from the Italian Parliament with a very large majority. In the Chamber of Deputies, 382 votes were cast in Orlando's favour and only 40 votes against (by the Socialists). During Orlando's absence, the Peace Conference continued – and probably even accelerated its work. When Orlando returned to Paris on 7 May 1919, the Conference was virtually over.

Keynes mentioned this episode briefly as an example of a minor matter about which the American President – whom he characterized as 'essentially theological, not intellectual' – could be roused to the fight. In *ECP*, Keynes wrote as follows about Wilson's style:

> A moment often arrives when substantial victory is yours if by some slight appearance of a concession you can save the face of the opposition or conciliate them by a restatement of your proposal helpful to them and not injurious to anything essential to yourself. The President was not equipped with this simple and usual artfulness. His mind was too slow and unresourceful to be ready with *any* alternatives (emphasis in the original). The president was capable of digging his toes in and refusing to budge, as he did over Fiume. But he had no other mode of defence, and it needed as a rule but little manoeuvring by his opponents to prevent matters from coming to such a head until it was too late (*ECP*, JMK, Vol II, p. 27).

Keynes offered his assessment of the damage to Italy arising from the absence of its delegation from the Peace Conference in a letter of 4 May 1919. Writing to the British Chancellor of the Exchequer, Lord Bradbury, he described the terms then arrived at by the Three and added: 'Up to the present the decision is secret and has been chiefly made, I imagine, as a reprisal against Italy. Italy's absence from the Conference will have cost her dear and her rage when she discovers what has happened during her absence will be correspondingly great' (JMK, XVI, p. 452).

Inevitably the Peace Treaty generated resentments in Italy. There were, of course, differences of opinion, but the general feeling was that the country had actually been defeated. Some years later, it was on those very feelings that Mussolini could build the myth of the 'crippled victory', a victory on the battlefields that had been turned into defeat at the tables of the Peace Conference. Subsequently, the Fascists invoked this myth to justify Mussolini's 'imperialist' policy.

While *ECP* struck a responsive chord in Italy between 1919 and 1921, reactions to the book took different forms. In the first instance, an important distinction must be drawn between the positions of two groups: between those who had favoured Italian intervention in the war and those who had opposed it. The most vociferous component of the latter group was the Socialist party (whose parliamentary strength, as noted earlier, was quite limited). Its spokesmen argued that the Peace Treaty demonstrated the soundness of their support for neutrality. The Socialists liked *ECP* very much. A Socialist leader, Claudio Treves, was later to introduce Keynes's *The Revision of the Treaty* to Italian audiences.

The pro-interventionist group was fairly homogeneous in its views, apart from a small minority which considered Italian intervention in the war as based on a 'democratic approach' to national and international issues, rather than on territorial claims. An interesting expression of the 'democratic approach' to intervention was made by Antonio de Viti de Marco, a leading public finance scholar, who found little to complain about in the Versailles Treaty. He was not pleased about the disposition of Fiume, which he thought should be recognized as part of Italy. But, in his view, the main objective of the war – that is, the elimination of a militaristic dictatorship – having been reached, it was incorrect to say, as indeed the Socialists were arguing, that the Paris Conference had led to an 'imperialist peace'.

On the other hand, a large majority of the 'interventionists' insisted that Italy deserved a larger share of the spoils of war on grounds that it had suffered, in proportion to the human and material resources of its economy, more harm than any other country in the winning coalition. They accepted the nationalistic narrow-mindedness displayed by the main European powers in Paris – and depicted by Keynes in *ECP* – as a fact of life. Accordingly, a settlement more consistent with Italian interests was appropriate. In *ECP*, Keynes had given only passing treatment to the Fiume question – the issue which most Italians regarded as the dramatic one. Even so, most 'interventionists' could associate themselves with Keynes's indictment of the way negotiations had been conducted in Paris; it served to reinforce their criticisms of a Treaty which was generally considered to be unjust to Italy. The critique developed by the 'interventionists', however, did not coincide with the one presented by Keynes. Their dissatisfaction with the outcome in Paris was based on disappointed territorial claims, not on monetary payments (the amount of which, in any case, would have been quite modest).

In February 1920, Keynes wrote quite triumphantly from England to an American acquaintance, 'Over here matters are moving quite fast and it is hardly an exaggeration to say that my main conclusions are now disputed by no one. Italy I hear is almost as free from illusion [of financial advantages] as England is rapidly becoming. I wish the same could be said of France' (JMK, Vol. XVII, p. 151). He did not seem to realize that the Italian public – which had never attached much importance to the reparations issue – had formed its views quite independently from the arguments of his book.

Commentators from Italian political life were not at one in their appraisals of the Treaty. But, despite divergent interpretations of the work of the Paris Conference, they could converge – although for quite different reasons – in finding something to applaud in Keynes's *ECP*.

II

One might have expected the reviewers of *ECP,* many of whom were professional economists, to address the technical arguments of the book more directly than the political commentators had done. In fact, however, most spoke from political positions with which they were already associated and did not examine in detail Keynes's economic argument on the non-feasibility of reparations.

One of the first Italian reviewers of *ECP* was Claudio Treves. In an essay entitled 'Al potere!' (Into Power), published in January 1920 in *Critica Sociale* (the Socialist fortnightly review), he blamed the capitalist and militaristic classes for causing the war, arguing that the working class would be 'naturally pacifist' if it had held political power. He maintained that *ECP* could be seen as a denunciation – analogous to the one made by the Socialist party – of the irresponsible behaviour of the capitalist system. The only way to implement a programme for a peaceful world – which would include, as Keynes had suggested, the elimination of inter-Allied indebtedness – would be the proletarian revolution. When Keynes published *A Revision of the Treaty* in January 1922, the Socialists immediately had it translated into Italian. Treves prepared a preface which was published in advance of the translation in *Critica Sociale* in April 1922. He took this opportunity to attack 'the old individualism' and to call for an internationalist approach. He accepted Keynes's main suggestions for reducing German indemnities, but did not discuss them systematically.

The Socialist fortnightly review took up the issue again in June 1921. Cesare Spellanzon, a professor who later gained fame as an historian of the Risorgimento, then published two articles on France and the question of German reparations in *Critica Sociale*. He supported the Keynesian approach entirely.

The *ECP* was also reviewed sympathetically by Luigi Einaudi, a highly regarded economist and political commentator. (Einaudi had entered the Italian Senate in 1919 and was subsequently to become a leading opponent of Fascism; after the Second World War, he became President of Italy.) Writing in *Il Corriere della Sera* on 15 February 1920, he observed that the book questioned both the wisdom and the justice of the Treaty. Einaudi's commentary referred to Keynes's discussion of the role of the Italian Prime Minister in the Fiume episode. But he also presented a broader account of Keynes's perspective:

> The author is not a German anxious about the future of his country, he is not an Italian eager to blame the inexperience of his representatives or Wilson's stubbornness for the difficulties faced on the issue of Fiume; nor is he a socialist who condemns the Treaty of Versailles as the fruit of imperialist and capitalist egoisms. He is an Englishman who feels that the Treaty cannot be implemented and who would have liked to translate Wilson's principles into a positive wording (Einaudi, 1921, pp. 239–50).

Einaudi's references to the economic aspects of the reparations question were, however, vague and general. In view of his role as an influential opinion-maker, it is reasonable to assume that his views on Keynes were widely shared. (It is worth noting that in 1915, Einaudi had been a firm interventionist. His arguments in favour of the war, as expressed in 'Guerra ed Economia,' *La Riforma Sociale*, June 1915, were quite moderate and not very far from those Antonio de Viti de Marco of the 'democratic group' in emphasizing the necessity to fight against imperialism.)

Other reviews included one signed V. P. (Vincenzo Porri, quite a well known economist) which appeared in 1920 in *La Riforma Sociale,* an economic journal edited by Einaudi, but it did not press the discussion beyond where Einaudi had taken it. The same journal published a more extensive review article by Giovanni di Modica in 1921. This review, polemically entitled 'The Economic Consequences of the War', agreed with Keynes's basic contention about revision of the Treaty, although the author claimed to have come to this position some time before the publication of *ECP*. Di Modica maintained, however, that *ECP*, in spite of its sound arguments against the Treaty, contained no suggestions for the reconstruction of the international system. In 1921, *La Riforma Sociale* also ran a short note announcing the publication of an Italian translation of *ECP*.

The contents of *ECP* were well summarized and its proposals endorsed in a review appearing in *Rivista Internazionale di Scienze Sociali e Discipline*

Ausiliarie (May–June 1920, pp. 95–7). The reviewer, Lanfranco Maroi, was a well known statistician: Keynes had referred to Maroi's book on the measurement of national wealth when evaluating 'legitimate claims' to indemnities in *ECP* (Maroi, 1919, in JMK, II, p. 84). Similar treatment was accorded to *ECP* in *Il Giornale degli Economisti* (May–June 1920, pp. 507–8), and again in *Rivista Internazionale di Scienze Sociali e Discipline Ausiliarie* (Grilli, 1920, pp. 178–98).

Keynes's book clearly attracted considerable attention among scholars, even before the appearance of the Italian edition in 1921. But the commentary on the technical economic arguments bearing on the feasibility of reparations was generally slight.

III

Special mention should be made of the analysis of *ECP* made by Francesco Saverio Nitti, a professor of public finance who served as Prime Minister of Italy in 1919–20. As minister of the Treasury in the Orlando cabinet, Nitti had intended to take part in the Paris Conference. Because of the opposition of the minister of foreign affairs to his participation, he resigned just before the Conference began. In October 1919 – as prime minister – he issued a statement describing the budgetary situation in Italy which Keynes reported in *ECP*, as an illustration of the post-war financial difficulties experienced by European belligerents.[2]

In 1921 and 1922, Nitti published a trilogy offering great insight into the actual and prospective situation in Europe. These volumes were soon translated into many languages, including English. In the first, *Europa senza Pace* (*Peaceless Europe*), he surveyed the international situation, including the reparations issue, and his comments on *ECP* in that context were by far the most penetrating of any to be offered by Italians.[3] Nitti and Keynes had common convictions. Nitti's estimates, however, of the indemnities that could be paid by Germany were lower than those made by Keynes. Nitti proposed that the needed revision of the Treaty should be negotiated through the auspices of the League of Nations – and with the defeated countries participating – to establish a truly balanced international system.

Keynes warmly reviewed Nitti's second volume – *La Decadenza dell' Europa* (*The Decadence of Europe*) – for *The Times* of London in January 1923. He commended the author for his 'outspokenness' and for his refusal 'to propound one more of those ingenious half-solutions which try to build up on the existing foundations. He regards the Treaty of Versailles as a piece of savagery incompatible with civilisation. He demands that we make a new beginning....' Keynes took exception on one point. He did 'not altogether share the author's pessimism. The battle of opinion is already much more nearly won than he seems to think' (JMK, XVIII, pp. 113–15). Both Nitti and Keynes were among the nominees for the Nobel Peace Prize in 1923.

The dissatisfaction of the Italians of all political persuasions with the results of the Paris Conference had produced a receptive audience for part of the message of Keynes's *ECP*. But with only few prominent exceptions – Nitti being a case in point – it was welcomed as a reinforcement to Italian political grievances, not as a contribution to debate on economic issues.

Notes
1.   JMK refers to *The Collected Writings of John Maynard Keynes*.
2.   Keynes referred to Nitti in *ECP*, JMK, Vol. II, p. 156.
3.   A complete picture of Italian views about the Peace Conference and its outcomes is provided in an article by P. Pastorelli, 'Politica Estera e Maggioranze Parlamentari, da Versailles a Rapallo' in *Il Parlamento Italiano*, Milano: Nuova Cei Information, Vol. IX (1988), pp. 177–200.

References
Einaudi, L. (1921), 'Come si giunse al Trattato di Versailles', reprinted in L. Einaudi, *Gli Ideali di un Economista*, Florence: La Voce.

Grilli, C. (1920), 'La Ricostruzione Economia e Sociale in Recenti Pubblicazione', *Rivista Internazionale di Scienze Sociale e Discipline Ausiliare*, November.

Keynes, J.M. (1919), 'The Economic Consequences of the Peace', reprinted in *The Collected Writings of John Maynard Keynes*, Vol II (1971), London: Macmillan.

Keynes, J.M. (1922), 'A Revision of the Treaty' in *The Collected Writings of John Maynard Keynes*, Vol III (1971), London: Macmillan.

Keynes, J.M. (1971–1989), *The Collected Writings of John Maynard Keynes*, London: Macmillan.

Nitti, F.S. (1921), *Peaceless Europe*, London: Cassell and Company.

Maroi, L. (1919), 'Come Si Calcola e a Quanto Ammonta la Ricchezza d'Italia e delle Altre Principali Nazioni' in *The Collected Works of John Maynard Keynes*, Vol II (1971), London: Macmillan.

di Viti de Marco, A. (1930), *Un Trentennio di Lotte Politiche*, Rome: Collezione Medidionale Editrice.

PART III

CRITIQUES OF THE KEYNESIAN PERSPECTIVE

6 The debate between Hayek and Keynes

Gilles Dostaler[1]

The three decades following the Second World War witnessed the domination, in economic policy as well as in economic theory, of what is loosely called Keynesianism. This domination has since been challenged by monetarism and the so-called new classical macroeconomics. All these expressions refer to complex movements of ideas. But there has been, since the beginning of the 1970s, a general trend away from the few theoretical and political underpinnings that form the core of all variants of Keynesianism, such as the primacy of investment over saving and the necessity of stabilization policies. The award of the Nobel Memorial Prize in Economics to Friedrich Hayek in 1974 may be considered as a symbol of this movement. Neither Hayek nor the Austrian school has officially occupied a leading role in theory or in politics. The word 'Hayekism' is not often heard, and 'Austrian school' sounds a bit old-fashioned. But Hayek's long struggle against Keynesianism, his defence of unfettered liberalism, in his writings as well as in his actions, has still had great influence on actual events. All of the concrete details of the neo-liberal agenda can be found in Hayek's writings of thirty and forty years ago. Some theoreticians of the new classical macroeconomics recognize him as an ancestor. However, the victory is far from complete, witness the current emergence of a new Keynesianism. This is one of the reasons why reconsideration of the debate between John Maynard Keynes and Friedrich Hayek, which took place between 1925 and 1946, is more timely than ever. It resonates with the main controversies of our day, not only in economic theory, but in politics, morals and social philosophy.

Space precludes treatment of all aspects of the debate between Keynes and Hayek. Both authors are more than mere economists. Their economic thought is rooted in philosophy, ethics and epistemology. Keynes's and Hayek's first important writings were concerned with philosophy.[2] Even in his most recent book, *The Fatal Conceit* (1988), Hayek insisted on a profound gulf between his vision of ethics and Keynes's, as expressed especially in the latter's 'My Early Beliefs', where Keynes defined himself as an immoralist.[3]

The following pages concentrate on the economic aspect of the debate, from Hayek's first attack on Keynes's economic vision, in 1925, to their last exchanges just before Keynes's death, in 1946. We shall examine in particular the battle that took place in the few years following the publication of Keynes's

A Treatise on Money in 1930 (JMK, V and VI) and Hayek's *Prices and Pro-duction* (Hayek, 1931a). In the early 1930s Hayek's theory represented a real challenge to Keynes. Moreover, Hayek's criticisms contributed in an important way to developments that led to *The General Theory of Employment, Interest and Money*, in 1936 (JMK, VII). As is well known, the publication of that book produced the era of Keynesian supremacy. But it was still not a definitive victory, as the latest developments show. A careful account of the earlier battle is thus useful in shedding light, not only on the history of economics in the 1930s, but on contemporary debates in macroeconomics as well.

The first exchanges
The debate between Hayek and Keynes started at the beginning of Hayek's career as a economist. One of his first articles, written after a stay in the United States, was entitled 'The Monetary Policy of the United States after the Recovery from the 1920 Crisis' (Hayek, 1925). The theoretical core of this paper was concerned with the attempts to influence the level of economic activity by banking policy, of which Hayek was already very critical. Keynes had published *A Tract on Monetary Reform* in 1923 (JMK, IV) and started his work on *A Treatise on Money*. Hayek here mentioned Keynes as an advocate in England, as Fisher was in the United States, of the new concept of monetary stabilization of the general price level. This was a mistake, in Hayek's view, because 'the cyclical movement finds its initial expression not in the behaviour of the general price level but in that of the relative prices of the individual groups of commodities' (Hayek, 1925, p. 17). Hayek noted that the old Currency school had already, more than one hundred years before, developed a true understanding of these phenomena. Thus, from the beginning, the differences between Hayek and Keynes appeared as a continuation of those that had divided the Currency school from the Banking school, and even before that, the Bullionists from their critics. The gist of the trade cycle theory that Hayek was to develop in the following years was already contained in a note to this article:

> Since the interest on capital – as all modern (catallactic) theories agree – represents the necessary limit to a disproportionate expansion of the capitalistic mode of production, an interest rate which is temporarily too low must give rise to an excessive accumulation of capital. This would be equivalent to an ever-intensifying widening of the basis of the pyramid of the capitalistic structure of the economy while the savings necessary to raise its height are not available (Hayek, 1925, p. 28).

Keynes and Hayek met for the first time in 1928. Many years later, Hayek recalled that 'though we had at once our first strong disagreement on some point of interest theory, we remained thereafter friends who had many interests in common, although we rarely could agree on economics' (Hayek, 1978, p. 283).

Of his new friend, Hayek added that 'if someone stood up to him he would respect him forever afterwards even if he disagreed' (ibid.). He had the impression that Keynes was principally led by aesthetic and intuitive factors rather than by rational considerations, even in the domain of economics. 'He was, by gift and temperament, more an artist and politician than a scholar or student' (p. 287).

That same year, Hayek published, in German, an important article, 'Intertemporal Price Equilibrium and Movements in the Value of Money', which contained the core of his analysis of the trade cycle and the foundations for his criticism of Keynes's theory. It is not surprising that Keynes and Hayek had their first strong verbal dispute on a point of interest theory. Hayek wrote that this article 'is intended to form part of a hitherto uncompleted larger work on the goals of monetary policy, which concentrates upon the analysis of the demand often voiced for an artificial stabilization of the "price level" with the means available to monetary policy' (Hayek, 1928, p. 113).

Part of this larger work was published in German in 1929, under the title *Monetary Theory and the Trade Cycle* (Hayek, 1933). As the gulf between Hayek's and Keynes's positions was soon to deepen, and the tone of their debate to become more acrimonious, it is worth emphasizing that in these early works we can still find, at a methodological level, some striking convergences between Keynes's and Hayek's positions. These convergences were rooted in their previous works on methodological and philosophical questions, as applied to probability for Keynes and to psychology for Hayek. Thus the first sentence of Hayek's 1928 article read: 'All economic activity is carried out through time' (Hayek, 1928, p. 71). For Keynes and Hayek, there was a close relationship between the consideration of time and money. At the close of this text, Hayek insisted on the difference between a barter economy and a monetary economy, in terms similar to those used by Keynes. He wrote that the task for him was 'to come to terms with the idea that money always exerts a determining influence on the development of the economy, that the principles derived for an economy without money can be applied to an economy with money only with substantial qualifications' (p. 103).

In the first chapter of *Monetary Theory and the Trade Cycle,* Hayek forcibly argued that one cannot use statistics to prove one's business cycle theory. Statistics can at most be utilized to falsify a theory: 'It is therefore only in a negative sense that it is possible to verify theory by statistics.... It cannot be expected to confirm the theory in positive sense' (Hayek, 1933, p. 34). Some years before, Keynes wrote in *A Treatise on Probability* that 'the hope, which sustained many investigators in the course of the nineteenth century, of gradually bringing the moral sciences under the sway of mathematical reasoning, steadily recedes – if we mean, as they meant, by mathematics the introduction of precise numerical methods' (JMK, VIII, p. 349). These ideas were to be reiterated in *The General Theory,* as well as in the 1937 *Quarterly Journal of Economics* article (JMK, XIV, pp. 109–23) and his subsequent debate with Tinbergen (JMK, XIV, pp. 285–320). The importance of expectations and uncertainty was underlined by the two authors in many places. It formed one of the foundations of their often similar criticisms of what Keynes called 'classical' theory and what Hayek sometimes called the 'current' theory.[4] It is not surprising to read, in Keynes's *Treatise on Money,* that among the few economists who developed theories similar to his own was Friedrich Hayek. But at the same time, it was with the publication of this book that hostilities began. Before describing this phase of the debate, we shall first summarize both authors' theories, as they were formulated at the beginning of the 1930s.

The weapons

Hayek's theory
The first version of Hayek's theory of trade cycles was presented to the public in the above mentioned article and in *Monetary Theory and the Trade Cycle.* In February 1931, three months after the publication of Keynes's *Treatise on Money,* Hayek was invited to give a series of lectures at the London School of Economics, where he was to be offered a post and to remain until 1950. These lectures were published in September 1931 under the title *Prices and Production* (Hayek, 1931a). Hayek considered this book as the logical sequel to *Monetary Theory and the Trade Cycle.* Moreover, it set out the fundamental doctrine to which Hayek was to remain committed. As late as 1975, in a preface to the French translation of *Prices and Production*, Hayek wrote that he still believed that his 1931 theory was the correct explanation of the crisis and that the errors of the previous forty years would have been avoided if he – rather than Keynes – had been listened to.[5]

Hayek's thesis was grounded in the Austrian or, more exactly, in the Jevons–Böhm-Bawerk theory of capital. In this vision, capital was considered neither as a permanent fund, nor as a fixed factor of production. Capital was the whole of the renewable resources used in the process of producing final consumption goods. Capital goods, as well as consumption goods, were ultimately the product of labour and natural resources. The crucial element was time – the distance between an act of production and final consumption. A central aspect of this approach was the temporal structure of production and the idea of stages of production (which was later transformed into the concept of the investment period). In this scheme of things, investment signified a lengthening of the structure of production, an increase in the so-called 'roundaboutness' of the production process. In equilibrium, the structure of production was determined by the choices of the agents between immediate and future consumption – that is, between current consumption and voluntary saving. This equilibrium reflected a given structure of relative prices. The relative prices, including the rate of interest, were the signals to which entrepreneurs responded in determining which structure of production should prevail. A reduction of the actual rate of interest (the Wicksellian monetary rate) below the equilibrium rate (the Wicksellian natural or real rate) had the effect of lengthening artificially the structure of production. This is what Hayek called overinvestment. An artificial stimulus to investment, in turn, created a disequilibrium between voluntary saving and investment which produced disequilibrium in the structure of production. Overinvestment was rendered possible by what Hayek called 'forced saving'.

'Forced saving' was obviously the antithesis of 'voluntary saving'. When the latter occurred, savers willingly released resources to finance investment and an equilibrium could be achieved automatically. But a different mechanism was brought into play when investment was stimulated artificially. Claims on real resources would still have to be surrendered to permit real capital formation to proceed, but in this case real consumption would have to be suppressed and real saving increased involuntarily. This result would be accomplished through increased prices of consumption goods which would shrink the claims on real resources of consumers with fixed incomes.

'Forced saving', however, could only continue with ever increasing inflation. At some point, the source of forced saving would disappear, the process would be reversed and a 'crisis' would ensue. Indeed the crisis was the only way to correct the distortion in the structure of production caused by an artificial stimulation of investment. In Hayek's view, it followed that any attempt to cure depression by extending artificial stimulation through credit expansion could only aggravate the depression.

A Treatise on Money

The theoretical kernel of Keynes's *Treatise* is to be found in the third and fourth books in which he developed his fundamental equations, linking the price level to the rate of efficiency earnings of the factors of production and the discrepancy between saving and investment. These differences were related to the existence of windfall profits or losses, which Keynes excluded from his definition of income. National income included only what he called the normal profits of the entrepreneurs. He also distinguished between receipts from the sale of investment goods (I) and the costs of these goods (I'). Saving, S, was defined as the difference between receipts (with the exception of windfall profits or losses), E, and consumption expenditures, R. The price level of consumption goods was proportional to their cost of production, which he called the rates of efficiency earnings, and to the differences between I' and S. The general level of prices was proportional to the given rates of efficiency earnings, but also to the difference between *I* and *S* (JMK, V, pp. 122–3.)

The difference between investment (measured by its price or its cost) and saving was the key factor in the explanation of price fluctuations, given that the rates of earnings moved slowly and could not be modified by decree, 'as in Bolschevist Russia or in Fascist Italy' (p. 244). Discrepancy between saving and investment finally explained what Keynes then called the 'credit cycle'. He added that one could find in the works of Mises, Schumpeter and Robertson a similar distinction between saving and investment. Saving was 'the act of the individual consumer and consists in the negative act of refraining from spending the whole of his current income on consumption', while investment, which is not necessarily equal to it, was 'the act of the entrepreneur whose function it is to make the decisions which determine the amount of the non-available output, and consists in the positive act of starting or maintaining some process of production or of withholding liquid goods. It is measured by the net addition to wealth whether in the form of fixed capital, working capital or liquid capital' (p. 155).

Thus far there was little distance between Keynes and Hayek. Both acknowledged the influence of Wicksell. Of Wicksell's *Geldzins und Güterpreise*, Keynes wrote that it 'deserves more fame and much more attention than it has received from English-speaking economists. In substance and intention Wicksell's theory is closely akin... to the theory of this treatise' (p. 167). Keynes then spoke of a German and an Austrian school of thought, which might be called neo-Wicksellian, that was in fact very close to his ideas as developed in the *Treatise*. He mentioned Ludwig von Mises, Hans Neisser and Friedrich Hayek (whose *Monetary Theory and the Trade Cycle* he had read in German).

The explicit differences between Keynes and Hayek lay in their respective definitions of the two terms, saving and investment. Keynes eventually abandoned the definitions developed in the *Treatise*, probably prompted by criticisms from Hayek and others. But there was a more profound implicit divergence which concerned the links of causality between the realities these terms imply and their combination in the process which leads to the crisis. With respect to Hayek's analysis, we can say the crisis was explained by the insufficiency of saving (even though Hayek preferred the expression 'overinvestment' because saving was at the right level when determined by the time preferences of agents). In a brief section of his book, Keynes examined those theorists who explained crisis by oversaving or underconsumption. He mentioned Bounatian, Hobson, Foster and Catchings, adding: 'At bottom these theories have, I think, some affinity to my own' (JMK, V, p. 160). Hayek had already made clear his objections to this body of doctrine. In a long article first published in German in 1929 and then in English in 1931, Hayek criticized Foster and Catchings at length, calling them 'purchasing power theorists' and pointing to the danger of the 'new theory of under-consumption now current in the United States and in England' (Hayek, 1931d, p. 126). He added that arguments asserting 'that saving renders the purchasing power of the consumer insufficient to take up the volume of current production...is almost as old as the science of political economy itself' (Hayek, 1931d, p. 125), mentioning the Mercantilists, Lauderdale, Malthus and the Socialists.

For Keynes, in the *Treatise* as in the rest of his work, it was clear that investment was the active mainspring of prosperity and growth, in the short run as well as in the long run, even if artificially stimulated against the advice of those he called the 'puritans of finance' (JMK, V, p. 246). The key to prosperity lay in the control of the level of investment: 'the art of management of money consists partly in devising technical methods by which the central authority can be put in a position to exercise a sensitive control over the rate of investment' (JMK, VI, pp. 189–90). Like Hayek, Keynes wrote that credit stimulated the boom. But unlike Hayek, he did not believe that it would sooner or later provoke a reversal. Many other causes could be identified, such as 'the evaporation of the attractions of new investment, the faltering of financial sentiment, the reaction in the price level of consumption goods, and the growing inability of the banking system to keep pace with the increasing requirements, first of the industrial circulation and later of the financial circulation also' (JMK, V, 273).

In Chapter 30 of Book 6, a digression entitled 'Historical Illustrations', the gulf between the two visions most clearly appeared. Here Keynes explained how, from the early stages of economic growth in the ancient world, there were two main factors of growth. The first was the availability of liquidity; the other was enterprise. Enterprise needed attractive profit expectations and appropriate behaviour of the financial and banking system. Thrift played no role, or rather a negative role, in that game. The accumulation rate was in no way linked to thrift habits: '... the increment of wealth coming wholly out of increased activity and not out of diminished consumption; not to mention the augmentation of real income, due to this increment of capital, in succeeding years. Were the seven wonders of the world built by thrift? I deem it doubtful' (JMK, VI, pp. 133–4). Hayek surely inspired the school of thought about which Keynes wrote as follows:

> In Great Britain especially there has been a school of thought which has believed that the way to bring down the rate of interest in the long run ... is to stimulate saving by a thrift campaign whilst simultaneously putting obstacles in the way of invest-ment by an 'economy' campaign – oblivious of the fact that savings which are not invested are spilt and add nothing to the national wealth. It is *investment*, i.e. the increased production of material wealth in the shape of capital goods, which alone in the long run brings down the natural rate of interest (JMK, VI, p. 185–6; Keynes's emphasis).

The battle

Hayek's first assault

Hayek's review of *A Treatise on Money* was his longest systematic criticism of Keynes's thesis. It appeared in *Economica* in two parts, in August 1931 (Hayek, 1931b) and in February 1932 (Hayek, 1932a). Keynes's reply (JMK, XIII, pp. 243–56) and a rejoinder by Hayek appeared in November 1931 (Hayek, 1931c). Hayek's text consisted of 50 densely-printed pages, divided into 18 sections. In the first part of his article, published at the same time as his *Prices and Production*, Hayek referred the reader to the second and third chapters of his book, presented as an alternative theory with 'a broad outline of the general theoretical considerations which seem to me indispensable in any approach to this problem' (Hayek, 1931b, p. 271). Hayek's criticism referred exclusively to the third and fourth books of Keynes's *Treatise*. The first article discussed the theoretical foundation, while the second proposed to deal with practical applications.

In the first article, Hayek's main critique addressed Keynes's definitions, or what he called his confused terminology. This, he suggested, was due to the fact that the work represented a transitional phase in a process of rapid intellectual development and that Keynes had been in a hurry to publish his provisional results for political reasons. In Hayek's judgement, this made reading the book extremely difficult: it was obscure, non-systematic and its argumentation often very weak.

The first problem arose from the definition of profits, which Hayek considered to be of a purely monetary nature in Keynes's theory. More generally, 'throughout the whole of his argument the flow of money is treated as if it were the only independent variable which could cause a positive or negative difference between the prices of the products and their respective costs' (p. 273). We have here one of the main bones of contention between Keynes and Hayek. Even though money mattered for both, it entered their systems in quite different ways. Hayek did not agree that the variations in profits, as defined by Keynes, were the only causes of expansion or reduction of production. Profits might result from sources other than the discrepancies between current receipts and current expenditures: for example, from variations in the value of existing capital goods.

Hayek maintained that Keynes did not explain the true origin of profits. To this was linked the confusion in the definition of investment: 'its meaning is constantly shifting between the idea of any surplus beyond the reproduction of the identical capital goods which have been used up in current production and the idea of any addition to the total value of the capital goods' (p. 274). The absence of a clear concept of investment was further related to an artificial separation between capitalist and entrepreneur, another central concept of

Keynes's analysis.

For Hayek, the obscurity and weakness of Keynes's analysis of investment arose from a misunderstanding of a correct theory of capital, such as that developed by Böhm-Bawerk. Although Keynes presented himself as a disciple of Wicksell, Hayek charged that 'Mr. Keynes ignores completely the general theoretical basis of Wicksell's theory' (p. 279). An inadequate analysis of capital led to ambiguities. As Hayek put it:

> These obscurities are not a matter of minor importance. It is because he has allowed them to arise that Mr. Keynes fails to realise the necessity of dealing with the all-important problem of changes in the value of existing capital; and this failure, as we have already seen, is the main cause of this unsatisfactory treatment of profit. It is also partly responsible for the deficiencies of his concept of capital. I have tried hard to discover what Mr. Keynes means by investment by examining the use he makes of it, but all in vain (Hayek, 1931b, p. 281).

In the sixth part of his text, Hayek offered a diagrammatic presentation of Keynes's fundamental equations, which, he said, were very difficult to read because of Keynes's incoherent choice of symbols. Keynes was right when he first considered separately the division of income between that portion earned in the production of investment goods and that portion earned in the production of consumption goods, and second, the division between that portion spent on consumption goods and that portion spent on investment goods. Keynes saw, as did Hayek, that the discrepancies between saving and investment, or, in Wicksell's words, between the real and monetary rates of interest, were the crux of the matter: 'the new approach, which Mr. Keynes has adopted, which makes the rate of interest and its relation to the saving and investment the central problem of monetary theory ... directs the attention to what is really essential' (p. 270). But the decision of entrepreneurs about allocating money to the production of investment goods cannot be arbitrary; the analysis of what motivates them is a 'problem which can be solved only on the basis of a complete theory of capital' (p. 285).

Hayek then criticized the concept of the money rate of efficiency earnings of the factors of production. He insisted that, in Keynes's model, there was no market in which these rates would be determined. More fundamentally, Hayek did not see why, if investment and saving in Keynes's sense could be equal, price movement should depend on the contracts with the factors of production. Only variations in the quantity of money could lead to discrepancies between saving and investment. Hayek went so far as to write that this was fundamentally the position of Keynes. Keynes erred when thinking that the quantity of money could be adapted to contracts in place without disrupting the relations between saving and investment. Keynesianism is thus viewed as a 'monetary surrender' to the claims of workers' unions and to monopoly power:

> *The difference seems to lie in the fact that Mr. Keynes believes that it is possible to*
> *adapt the amount of money in circulation to what is necessary for the maintenance*
> *of existing contracts without upsetting the equilibrium between saving and invest-*
> *ing.* But under the existing monetary organisation, where all changes in the quantity
> of money in circulation are brought about by more or less money being lent to
> entrepreneurs than is being saved, any change in the circulation *must* be accom-
> panied by a divergence between saving and investing (Hayek, 1931b, pp. 292–3;
> Hayek's emphasis).

To summarize, Keynes was right to see in the divergences between saving and
investment (or between the natural and monetary rates of interest of Wicksell)
a very important phenomenon to account for contemporary economic difficulties. But his explanation of this phenomenon, and the relation he established in
his equations between it and the earnings of factors of production was incorrect.
Curiously enough, Hayek added that this shortcoming did not spoil what was
'undeniably in so many ways a magnificent performance' (p. 294). Hayek
acknowledged that perhaps he had not understood Keynes's thesis because of
terminological difficulties. This explained why he preferred to delay publication of the second part of his review. He allowed that clarification by Keynes
of certain ambiguities could lead to a spectacular result: 'It is even possible that
in the end it will turn out that there exists less difference between Mr. Keynes's
views and my own than I am at present inclined to assume' (p. 295). But that
was not the way the things turned out.

Keynes's counter-attack

Keynes reacted very strongly to Hayek's article, an indication of his sensitivity
to the attack. His copy of Hayek's piece contains no less than 34 marginal notes,
and ends with the following comment, which was not published:

> Hayek has not read my book with that measure of 'good will' which an author is
> entitled to expect of a reader. Until he can do so, he will not see what I mean or know
> whether I am right. He evidently has a passion which leads him to pick on me, but
> I am left wondering what this passion is (JMK, XIII, p. 243).

Keynes's reply was published in the November issue of *Economica*. Instead of
examining the possible convergences Hayek had called for at the end of his
article, Keynes concentrated on the 'abyss' between Hayek's thesis and his
own, which was already in a process of rapid transformation. This is why an
important part of his text was not a direct answer to Hayek's criticism of *A
Treatise on Money*, but instead a quite aggressive criticism of *Prices and
Production*, of which he wrote:

> The book, as it stands, seems to me to be one of the most frightful muddles I have
> ever read, with scarcely a sound proposition in it.... It is an extraordinary example
> of how, starting with a mistake, a remorseless logician can end up in Bedlam. Yet

Dr. Hayek has seen a vision, and though when he woke up he has made nonsense of his story by giving the wrong names to the objects which occur in it, his Khubla Khan is not without inspiration and must set the reader thinking with the germs of an idea in his head (JMK, XIII, p. 252).

Keynes accused Hayek of concentrating on absent or irrelevant terminological problems, without explaining why his conclusions were false. Moreover, he accused Hayek of totally misinterpreting his theory when writing, for example, that only a change in the quantity of money could lead to a divergence between investment and saving. But there was an important admission here. As Hayek and many others had made the same mistake when reading *A Treatise on Money*, Keynes recognized that part of the responsibility might lie with him:

Since Dr. Hayek has not been alone amongst competent critics of my *Treatise* in falling into this misapprehension ... I suspect that it may be partly due to the fact that when I first began to work on Book III of my *Treatise* I believed something resembling this myself. My ceasing to believe it was the critical point in my own development.... But traces of old trains of thought are not easily obliterated, and certain passages which I wrote some time ago, may have been unconsciously cast into a mould less obviously inconsistent with my own former views than they would be if I were writing now (JMK, XIII, pp . 246–7).

Keynes added that those, like Hayek, who are 'sufficiently steeped in the old point of view simply cannot bring themselves to believe that I am asking them to step in a new pair of trousers, and will insist on regarding it as nothing but an embroidered version of the old pair which they have been wearing for years' (p. 247). The new vision, Keynes maintained, was completely different from the old, which Hayek and others (such as Keynes's friend Robertson), accepted, along with all those whom he was later to call the 'classicals'. According to the old view, voluntary saving always found its way into investment, and so any disequilibrium between the two could only be the result of an action within the banking system. For Hayek, credit cycles could be avoided if the quantity of money were kept constant. The Keynesian perspective was diametrically opposed:

My analysis is quite different from this...in my view, saving and investment ... can get out of gear without any change on the part of the banking system from 'neutrality' as defined by Dr. Hayek, merely as a result of the public changing their rate of saving or the entrepreneurs changing their rate of investment, there being no automatic mechanism in the economic system...to keep the two rates equal, provided that the effective quantity of money is unchanged (JMK, XIII, p. 251; Keynes's emphasis).

Despite Keynes's belief that he and Hayek were living in different worlds, and that thousands of words of his would be 'water off a duck's back' for Hayek, Keynes confessed, in the end, not only verbal confusions, but also his lack of a satisfactory theory of capital and interest. He even admitted that one might possibly find in Böhm-Bawerk's theory foundations for developments that were absent from the *Treatise*. He conceded that his ideas on the determinants of the natural rate of interest were in an embryonic state and he promised to 'make good this deficiency' (p. 253). We now know that this was the route from the *Treatise* to *The General Theory,* in which the concepts of liquidity preference and marginal efficiency of capital were introduced and elaborated.

In a rejoinder, Hayek complained that Keynes had not eliminated the ambiguities he discovered and instead had condemned Hayek's thesis without a fair trial (Hayek, 1931c). No answer was given to Hayek's criticism of the definitions of profit and investment. No explanation was given for the discrepancies between saving and investment, or for Keynes's belief that there was no automatic mechanism to equilibrate them. Hayek pondered whether 'Mr. Keynes has ever reflected upon the function of the rate of interest in a society where there is no banking system' (p. 401). All this followed from the absence of an analysis of the fundamental non-monetary problems of capitalist economies, which, Hayek maintained, Keynes did not bother to analyse. He concluded by restating the old view, rejected by Keynes, on the causal relation between saving and investment:

> I think that if Mr. Keynes has for a moment reflected on what happens normally when saving increases and no special circumstances prevent investment from increasing at an equal rate ... he could not have failed to see that only special monetary factors ... could prevent such a change in saving from exerting a direct influence in the same direction on the rate of investing (Hayek, 1931c, pp. 402–3).

Hayek's second assault

In the second part of his critique, which appeared in the February 1932 issue of *Economica*, Hayek sharpened his criticism of Keynes's saving–investment apparatus. He repeated that he saw no proof, in Keynes's book, that the difference between the natural and effective rates of interest could be independent of variation in the effective circulation of money. For Wicksell, this situation was entirely caused by the elasticity of the monetary system, that is, by the possibility of adding or subtracting money from circulation.

Hayek felt that Keynes, like the majority of Anglo-Saxon economists, attached too much importance to the divergence between fixed and circulating capital, a fact that 'contributed more than any other cause to the unsatisfactory state of the English theory of capital at the present time' (Hayek, 1932a, p. 25). An unsatisfactory concept of investment was built on that basis, which then drove Keynes to a paradoxical conclusion that an increase in saving may not bring about an increase in investment. According to Hayek, Keynes derived this peculiar conclusion because of the particular definitions with which he began. Moreover, this had nothing to do with Wicksell, who could not be held responsible for Keynes's errors (p. 32).

In the last two sections of his long article, Hayek arrived at the core of his disagreement with Keynes. The hurried reader need examine only these, which are concerned with what Keynes called credit cycles. Here, Keynes was accused of disregarding the effects of monetary disequilibrium on real investment and of limiting himself to the study of 'shifts in the money streams and the consequent changes in the price level'.

> It seems never to have occurred to him that the artificial stimulus to investment, which makes it exceed current saving, may cause a dis-equilibrium in the real structure of production which, sooner or later, must lead to a reaction. Like so many others who hold a purely monetary theory of the trade cycle ... he seems to believe that, if the existing monetary organisation did not make it impossible, the boom could be perpetuated by indefinite inflation (Hayek, 1932a, p. 40).

Oddly enough, Hayek here credited Keynes with a pure, or naive, monetary vision of the economic process, in which only monetary flows were taken into account. Thus Keynes was considered as unable to understand how a situation of overinvestment could come about, and this led him to advocate, like underconsumption theorists, a stimulation of consumption expenditures to maintain expansion or combat depression, 'for, on his theory, the effects of cheap money and increased buying of consumers are equivalent' (p. 41). Within this theory, the excess of consumption goods demand over their cost constituted the boom which would last as long as demand was greater than supply:

> This seems to me to be, in broad outline, Mr. Keynes' explanation of the cycle. In essence it is not only relatively simple, but also much less different from the current explanations than its author seems to think; though it is, of course, much more complicated in its details. To me, however, it seems to suffer from exactly the same deficiencies as all the other, less elaborate, purchasing-power theories of the cycle (Hayek, 1932a, p. 41).

For a more elaborate criticism of these erroneous theories, Hayek referred to his *Prices and Production,* and his article 'The "Paradox" of Saving' (Hayek, 1931d). The deflation which accompanied the depression was not, according to Hayek, the cause of the depression. Rather, it was the real disequilibrium brought about by excess investment and inflation that provoked the reversal, or slowing down of economic activity and employment. For Hayek, Keynes failed to see that one cannot simultaneously increase the production of consumer goods and investment goods. He had displayed only a vague intuition of that profound truth. Had he followed his intuition, however, he would have discovered the true explanation of crisis (Hayek, 1932a, p. 42).

The only way out of the crisis was through the very long process of restoring the equilibrium destroyed during the boom. Any attempt to stimulate artificially by means of expanded credit was a false remedy that addressed symptoms rather than causes: 'Any attempt to combat the crisis by credit expansion will, therefore, not only be merely the treatment of symptoms as causes, but may also prolong the depression by delaying the inevitable real adjustments' (1932a, p. 44).

Negotiations and interventions of the troops

Keynes did not reply to Hayek's second article. The direct controversy between them ended with a letter, dated 29 March 1932, in which Keynes explained that he was now revising his thesis and could not waste too much time in discussion. All this was to be the matter of another book: 'I am trying to re-shape and improve my central position, and that is probably a better way to spend one's time than in controversy' (JMK, XIII, p. 266). Hayek, who said that he had put a lot of time into preparing his critiques, did not appreciate this response.

That letter marked the end of a correspondence which began on 10 December 1931, at Keynes's initiative. A careful reader of these letters may sometimes get the impression that Keynes was setting traps for Hayek. Keynes, for example, asked him to clarify his definitions of saving (forced and voluntary), of the velocity of circulation of money, of the 'maintenance of capital', of 'effective circulation'. Hayek's answer about forced saving written in December 1931, is worth quoting:

> I entirely agree with you that it would be better not to use the word saving in the connection with what I have called 'forced saving' but only to speak of investment in excess of saving. Unfortunately, however, the fact that you use 'saving' and 'investment' in a different sense has now made it difficult for me to adopt what is obviously the better terminology without creating confusion. It is essentially the different meaning of these concepts which is at the basis of our difference and it will be one of the main contentions of the second part of my article that while it is essential for an equilibrium that saving and investment in my sense should correspond, there seems to me to exist no reason whatever why saving and investment in your sense should correspond (JMK, XIII, p. 258).

One often gets a sense of a dialogue among the deaf. Keynes wrote to Sraffa and to Kahn on 1 February 1932: 'What is the next move? I feel that the abyss yawns – and so do I' (JMK, XIII, p. 265). Yet Keynes wrote to Hayek on 11 February that his answers helped him. However, he observed that the discussion could hardly continue productively by letter because it 'is obviously a matter for a book rather than for correspondence' (JMK, XIII, p. 265). He added that he had not really understood what seemed to be Hayek's main point, the difference between forced and voluntary saving.

There were many interventions by third parties in this struggle. Keynes's disciples of the 'Circus', such as Sraffa and Robinson, sided with their master, while Robertson and Hawtrey sided, at least partially, with Hayek. Many others were quite puzzled. Young economists at that time felt they had to choose between two rival theories, answering yes or no to the question as to whether or not buying a new overcoat in a period of depression would raise or lower unemployment. Richard Kahn had put this question to Hayek after the latter had delivered a lecture to the Marshall Society in Cambridge in 1931. Hayek had replied that the purchase of an overcoat would indeed raise unemployment but that 'it would take a very long mathematical argument to explain why' (Kahn, 1984, p. 182).

Thus there was, in the minds of many young economists at Cambridge, London and elsewhere, a struggle between Keynes's *Treatise* and Hayek's *Prices and Production*.[6] The final victory of *The General Theory* over Hayek's later works must not lead one to forget this important fact in the development of economic thought in the 1930s. This battle was not as simple as is often thought: Cambridge versus London School of Economics, Keynesianism versus classical or neo-classical theory, State intervention versus *laissez-faire*, or more simply left versus right. The situation was not so clear-cut. For example, many economists of the London School of Economics, then under the influence of Hayek and Robbins, were more to the left than many of Keynes's disciples and Keynes himself. Later in the 1930s, some left the Hayekian camp because of Hayek's political position, particularly when he began his crusade against 'collectivism' and planning.

John Hicks was one of the younger economists whose position in this debate was very difficult to classify. Based at the London School of Economics at that time, Hicks was close to Hayek and Robbins. But he was also influenced by Keynes's work. As is well known, he was one of the main proponents of the so-called 'Keynesian neo-classical synthesis'. However, he later became more and more critical of that mainstream Keynesianism. In an article entitled the 'Hayek Story', he later confessed his hesitations at the beginning of the 1930s:

> When the definitive history of economic analysis during the nineteen-thirties comes to be written, a leading character in the drama (it was quite a drama) will be Professor Hayek. ... it is hardly remembered that there was a time when the new theories of Hayek were the principal rival of the new theories of Keynes. Which was right, Keynes or Hayek? There are many still living teachers of economics and practical economists, who have passed through a time when they had to make up their minds on that question; and there are many of them (including the present writer) who took quite a time to make up their minds (Hicks, 1967, p. 203).

Some tried a synthesis. Nicholas Kaldor expressed this hope in a letter to Keynes in November 1931 (JMK, XIII, pp. 238–40). He was then a research student at the London School of Economics and was fascinated by the Austrian economist whose *Monetary Theory and the Trade Cycle* and 'The Paradox of Saving' he was to translate. Commenting on a debate between Keynes and Robertson, he wrote that a clarification by Keynes on some points could help to bridge the gap between these disparate points of view.

Among the younger economists, several attempts to bridge the gap between Cambridge and the London School of Economics were undertaken. One such move led to the founding of a new journal, *The Review of Economics Studies* (referred to by the elders as the 'Children's Magazine'), which was intended to provide a forum for discussion between graduate students at the two institutions. In addition, a weekend meeting was convened at Newport (between Cambridge and London) in August 1933 with Abba Lerner, Richard Kahn, James Meade, Joan and Austin Robinson in attendance.

But despite these testimonies of good will, some other exchanges were very harsh. The most violent attack on Hayek's theory was probably the one levelled by Sraffa in the March 1932 issue of *The Economic Journal*. Keynes, as editor of the journal, granted a reply to Hayek, but wrote to him, on March 29: 'But let it be no longer than it need be. It is the trouble of controversy – from an editor's point of view – that it is without end' (JMK, XIII, p. 266). In his reply, Hayek suggested that Sraffa did not seem to understand Keynes's theory. This led to an awkward situation. Keynes added a note to Hayek's article which read as follows: 'With Prof. Hayek's permission I should like to say that, to the best of my comprehension, Mr. Sraffa has understood my theory accurately' (in Hayek, 1932b, p. 249).

Joan Robinson also came to Keynes's rescue with 'A Parable on Savings and Investment', published in the February 1933 issue of *Economica*, addressed to 'the ordinary muddle-headed reader of economics, brought up in the Quantity Theory school who is suddenly presented with the argument of the *Treatise*' (Robinson, 1933, p. 75). Her intention was 'to state what seems to me the fundamental difficulty of such a reader in the simplest possible terms, leaving on one side all the subtleties and complications both of Dr. Hayek's and Mr. Keynes's arguments' (p. 75).

Dennis Robertson also intervened in what he described, in a letter to Keynes on 4 October 1931, as 'this 3-cornered debate, all of us talking different dialects' (JMK, XIII, p. 271). On 22 March 1932, Keynes sent Robertson a long note on the definitions of saving which sheds considerable light on his position as well as on his disagreements with Hayek, Robertson and Hawtrey. It is clear that the correspondence with Hayek had helped Keynes to clarify his own position on these questions. The main point was that investment is the causal factor, however saving and investment may be defined. Saving was not a virtue: '*I* [for investment] always drags *S'* [saving] along with it at an equal pace. *S'* is not the voluntary result of virtuous decisions. In fact *S'* is no longer the dog, which common sense believes it to be, but the tail' (JMK, XIII, p. 276).

It is worth noting that, while Keynes considered Hawtrey and Hayek to be in the same army, there was a lively indirect exchange between the two in the February 1932 issue of *Economica*. Hawtrey reviewed *Prices and Production* (Hawtrey, 1932)[7] and Hayek reviewed Hawtrey's *Trade Depression and the Way Out* (Hayek, 1932c). Hawtrey's criticism was severe, but not so much so as Sraffa's. For his part, Hayek described Hawtrey as belonging to that group which believed that the problems lay in the insufficiency of consumption goods demand. So, according to Hayek, Hawtrey and Keynes were in the same camp. All this illustrates the difficulties and perils associated with rigid classifications in economics. Alliances continuously change, depending on circumstances. At that time, Hayekians often became Keynesians and vice versa. And to complicate matters still further, Hayek and Keynes were sometimes allied against another army, for example, the army of formalists and mathematicians. In a review of business cycle theories, Tinbergen referred to Keynes's and Hayek's models as similar in structure, as they were both open models which could not be formalized mathematically. He contrasted these models to a group of closed models which could be written mathematically, such as those developed by Frisch and Kalecki (Tinbergen, 1935).

After *The General Theory*

The transition from the *Treatise* to *The General Theory* was described by Keynes as the way out of a dark tunnel, as some kind of 'illumination' like that of Saint Paul on the road to Damascus, or as a ceremony of catharsis. It is now clear that, apart from the 'Circus' discussions and other criticisms, the one by Hayek played a considerable role in Keynes's own clarification of his main thesis. Hayek was also severely criticized, and undertook to clarify, extend and transform his own thesis in a series of articles in which he constantly attacked 'monetary nationalists' and 'purchasing power theorists', of whom Keynes was for him the most distinguished representative.[8] He once wrote that this fight against the old fallacies, newly dressed, of underconsumption theories led him away from his task of the reconstruction of business cycle theories founded on a correct theory of capital and investment.

Keynes sent an advance copy of *The General Theory* to Hayek, who expressed his gratitude in a letter dated 2 February 1936, two days before the publication date. This letter is worth quoting at some length:

> I fully agree about the importance of the problem which you outline at the beginning, but I cannot agree that it has always been as completely neglected as you suggest.
> ...I am still puzzled by the treatment of the saving-investment relationship, of liquidity preference and some other points. But probably all that will be cleared up when I have worked through the whole systematically. But if my present doubts remain I shall probably ask for your hospitality for some notes on particular points in the E.J.

...even if I should ultimately find that I disagree on many points I have no doubt
that I shall have learnt a great deal and probably look in an entirely new light on
many problems (JMK, XXIX, pp. 207–8).

There was to be no comment by Hayek in *The Economic Journal,* nor any review of Keynes's book elsewhere. In later life, he severely blamed himself for
not having criticized this so-called 'General Theory' which was in fact 'too
obviously another tract for the times, conditioned by what he thought were the
momentary needs of policy' (Hayek, 1978, p. 284). The reason he did not do
so was his disappointment after his long criticism of the *Treatise,* when Keynes
told him 'that he had in the meantime changed his mind and no longer believed
what he had said in that work' (p. 284).

But Hayek's writings often alluded to Keynes's new theory. 'Utility Analysis and Interest' (Hayek, 1936) criticized the liquidity preference theory. In
Monetary Nationalism and International Stability in 1937, Hayek offered a
critique of Keynes's views on the determination of money and real wages:

> ... the working class would not be slow to learn that an engineered rise of prices is
> no less a reduction of wages than a deliberate cut of money wages, and that in
> consequence the belief that it is easier to reduce by the round-about method of
> depreciation the wages of all workers in a country than directly to reduce the money
> wages of those who are affected by a given change, will soon prove illusory (Hayek,
> 1937a, p. 53).

Even though Keynes's book was not explicitly mentioned, 'Investment that
Raises the Demand for Capital' in 1937 can be considered as Hayek's first
important answer to *The General Theory.* Hayek's intention was to give a new
formulation of what he called 'modern monetary overinvestment theories of the
trade cycle' (Hayek, 1937b, p. 73). He criticized the view according to which
the so-called 'marginal efficiency of capital' tended to decrease as investment
increased. On the contrary, an increase in capital could lead to an increase of
loanable funds.

But the real 'counter-attack' by Hayek was the publication, in 1939, of
Profits, Interest and Investment. This book contained his main articles on the
subject published since 1932, and a long previously unpublished text bearing
the same title as the book. The latter piece contained a new version of Hayek's
business cycle theory. He then used what he called the 'Ricardo effect',
according to which 'a rise in the price of the product (or a fall in real wages) will
lead to the use of relatively less machinery and other capital and of relatively
more direct labour in the production of any given quantity of output' (Hayek,
1939, p. 10). About mid-way through the recovery, real wages start to fall, as
prices of consumer goods rise. This leads to a shortening of the structure of
production, and therefore to a slow-down of production and a rise of unemployment in the capital goods industries. Hayek thus believed that he had shown

'that an increase in the demand for consumers' goods may lead to a decrease in the demand for capital goods' (p. 31). The end of the expansion period was always caused, in the last instance, by 'capital scarcity'. It was not brought about by a reduction in investment opportunities.

We are thus in a completely different universe from that of Keynes. There were only a few allusions to *The General Theory,* presented as one of the most influential attempts to make use of the thesis (nowhere demonstrated) that the demand for capital goods was derived from the demand for consumption goods. Hayek conceded that it was possible to stimulate employment in the short term by monetary policies. But this employment would be unstable, and the artificially created prosperity would breed future problems. This was the essence of Hayek's criticism of so-called Keynesian policies:

> But the economist should not conceal the fact that to aim at the maximum of employment which can be achieved in the short run by means of monetary policy is essentially the policy of the desperado who has nothing to lose and everything to gain from a short breathing space (Hayek, 1939, p. 64).

This line of critique was expanded in the last chapters of *The Pure Theory of Capital,* published in 1941. This was otherwise a very abstract book, concerned with the foundations of economic analysis, as its title indicated. Hayek set himself the very ambitious task of entirely reconstructing the theory of capital, and on that basis, of elaborating a correct theory of the business cycle. Only the first portion of this project was accomplished. Because of the war, Hayek decided to publish the material then at hand and did not return to the larger work. *The Pure Theory of Capital* can thus be regarded as his last work in pure economic theory. Hayek, from this time on, wrote mainly about philosophy, methodology, politics and the history of ideas.

The last part of *The Pure Theory of Capital,* beginning with Chapter 25, contains an explicit criticism of Keynes's theory as well as of Keynes's politics. The true origin of crisis, according to Hayek, stemmed from the fact that 'a community has started to live beyond its income' (Hayek, 1941, p. 348). This led inevitably to a cumulative process. Overconsumption was always the villain. The relative excess demand for consumer goods created a situation in which the irreversibility of time had the most serious consequences. The existence of excess demand was linked with government intervention and monopolistic extortions, by which Hayek meant a rise of wages enforced by workers' unions. This provoked a transfer of income from capitalists to other classes, which in turn raised consumer goods demand and diminished the funds available for investment.

Hayek believed that Keynes's theory, heir to a tradition dating back as far as John Law, was conceived for a society with an ample stock of unutilized resources. The universe of *The General Theory* 'which in recent years has created so much stir and confusion among economists and even the wider public' (p. 374) did not correspond to the present-day world:

> Although the technocrats, and other believers in the unbounded productive capacity of our economic system, do not yet appear to have realised it, what he has given us is really that economics of abundance for which they have been clamouring so long. Or rather, he has given us a system of economics which is based on the assumption that no real scarcity exists, and that the only scarcity with which we need concern ourselves is the artificial scarcity created by the determination of people not to sell their services and products below certain arbitrarily fixed prices (Hayek, 1941, p. 374).

Whatever the short term influence of monetary policies, 'it will in the end be the scarcity of real resources relative to demand which will decide what kind of investment, and how much, is profitable' (p. 393). This meant that 'ultimately, therefore, it is the rate of saving which sets the limits to the amount of investment that can be successfully carried through' (p. 393). To understand how this worked, the mechanism of prices was fundamental. There was no precise explanation in Keynes's book of the level of prices and of their variations. Thus its readers were not equipped to understand the complex relationships between costs, prices and profits which explained the choices of processes of production.

Keynes and his disciples, Hayek maintained, grossly overestimated 'the extent to which we can hope to shape events at will by controlling money' (p. 407). We cannot play as we wish with monetary instruments. Obviously, we cannot reject any kind of monetary policy 'since money by its very nature constitutes a kind of loose joint in the self-equilibrating apparatus of the price mechanism which is bound to impede its working' (p. 408). But the aims of such policies must be 'to reduce as far as possible this slack in the self-correcting forces of the price mechanism, and to make adaptation more prompt so as to reduce the necessity for a later, more violent, reaction' (p. 408). One must clearly distinguish the monetary façade from the real forces in action in the economic system. The fashionable doctrines neglecting the latter, which promised quick and happy results, were very dangerous. Nothing less than the future of civilization was at stake: 'I cannot help regarding the increasing concentration on short-run effects – which in this context amounts to the same thing as a concentration on purely monetary factors – not only as a serious and dangerous intellectual error, but as a betrayal of the main duty of the economist and a grave menace to our civilisation' (Hayek, 1941, p. 409).

Hayek added that two centuries of progress in economic theory helped us to look at the real forces beneath the monetary façade, but that Keynes and his friends wanted us to go back to the pre-scientific epoch of economics. Thus it was not surprising that Keynes rehabilitated the mercantilists, elevated to the dignity of science the short-view philosophy of the business man, and proclaimed that in the long run we are all dead: 'I fear that these believers in the principle of *après nous le deluge* may get what they have bargained for sooner than they wish' (Hayek, 1941, p. 410). In his last book,[9] Hayek forcefully repeated fifty years later the arguments of *The Pure Theory of Capital*, clearly linking his condemnation of Keynes's morals, economics and politics. One of the passages is worth quoting at length:

> This extraordinary man also characteristically justified some of his economic views, and his general belief in a management of the market order, on the ground that 'in the long run we are all dead' ... The slogan ... is also a characteristic manifestation of an unwillingness to recognise that morals are concerned with effects in the long run – effects *beyond our possible perception* – and of a tendency to spurn the learnt discipline of the long view.
>
> Keynes also argued against the moral tradition of the 'virtue of saving', refusing, along with thousands of crank economists, to admit that a reduction of the demand for consumers' goods is generally required to make an increase of the production of capital goods (i.e. investment) possible.
>
> And this in turn led him to devote his formidable intellectual powers to develop his 'general' theory of economics – to which we owe the unique world-wide inflation of the third quarter of our century and the inevitable consequence of severe unemployment that has followed (Hayek, 1988, pp. 57–8, emphasis in original).

The last exchanges

The only public exchanges between the two men following the publication of *The General Theory* occurred in a triangular discussion, involving F. D. Graham and his proposition of 'commodity reserve currency', in 1943 and 1944. Hayek was in favour of this proposition, which he considered a second best after the gold standard (Hayek, 1943). Keynes reiterated his positions of 1920 against the gold standard (Keynes, 1943). After an intervention by Graham (1944), who accused Keynes of paving the road to totalitarianism with his proposition, Keynes added that he doubted 'the political wisdom of appearing, more than is inevitable in any orderly system, to impose an external pressure on national standards and therefore on wage levels' (Keynes, 1944, pp. 429–30).

Keynes did not reply to the arguments developed in Hayek's books. As a matter of fact, Hayek's two books did not provoke any discussion at all comparable to that stimulated by the first one.[10] It was too late. The battlefield was then totally occupied by *The General Theory*. But Hayek did not get completely lost in a desert. Three years after his *Pure Theory of Capital,* he published a brief political book, dedicated 'to the socialists of all parties', *The Road to Serfdom* (Hayek, 1944). This was the book which made him world famous, as *The Economic Consequences of the Peace* (JMK, II), at the close of the First World War, had done for Keynes. The comparison can be pushed even further. The ideas expressed in these books, while not popular at the time of their publication, did exercise much more influence in the following decades.

But while Keynes had to wait about fifteen years, the purgatory was thirty years for Hayek.

Keynes read *The Road to Serfdom* while travelling to Bretton Woods. He wrote to Hayek from Atlantic City. This letter linked morals, politics and economics, and illustrates the complex relationships of convergences and divergences between the two authors. Of his friend's work, Keynes wrote that 'it is a grand book ... morally and philosophically I find myself in agreement with virtually the whole of it; and not only in agreement with it, but in a deeply moved agreement' (JMK, XXVII, p. 385). But Keynes did not accept 'quite all the economic dicta in it' (p. 385). The aims were the same for the two of them. But the means were quite different. Keynes insisted that one must avoid extremes and Hayek concurred. But, Keynes alleged, Hayek contradicted himself with his total rejection of any form of planning. For Keynes, what was needed to avoid totalitarianism was not less planning, but more.

> I should therefore conclude your theme rather differently. I should say that what we want is not no planning, or even less planning, indeed I should say that we almost certainly want more. But the planning should take place in a community in which as many people as possible, both leaders and followers, wholly share your own moral position (JMK, XXVII, p. 387).

Keynes went on to express his anxiety about the great danger ahead in 'the probable practical failure of the application of your philosophy in the U.S. in a fairly extreme form' (p. 387). He compared Hayek to a Don Quixote. We now know that Don Quixote's economic philosophy has prevailed after a lapse of thirty years. We are now in the domain of politics, and such was the subject of the last exchange between the two men, a few weeks before Keynes's death. According to Hayek, Keynes was by then moving in his direction:

> Indeed, I am fairly certain that if he had lived he would in that period have been one of the most determined fighters against inflation. About the last time I saw him, a few weeks before his death, he more or less plainly told me so. ... I had asked him whether he was not getting alarmed by the use of which some of his disciples were putting his theories. His reply was that these theories had been greatly needed in the 1930s; but if these theories should ever become harmful, I could be assured that he would quickly bring about a change in public opinion. What I blame him for is that he had called such a tract for the times the *General Theory* (Hayek, 1978, pp. 286–7).

Conclusion
Even if Keynes had lived longer, and changed his views to correspond with Hayek's hopes, we doubt that the gulf between their positions would have narrowed. Given their philosophical and political ideas, as well as the methodological foundations of their economics, they would always be opposed. There can hardly be any common ground between Hayek's conception

of capital, based on Böhm-Bawerk's thesis, and Keynes's vision. Their respective views of investment, saving and their relationship could not be reconciled. They were grounded in moral positions, as was quite clear from Hayek's latest writings.

This is an unending debate. It started more than two centuries ago, when Turgot and Smith elaborated the idea that any act of saving was an act of investment and that the private virtue of thrift was the mainspring of capital accumulation. According to that view, no government intervention was needed to guarantee the automatic macroeconomic adjustment at a full employment level. This supposition was constructed notwithstanding the conviction of many predecessors, such as Boisguilbert, Mandeville, Petty and Quesnay, some of whom said that the private vice of spendthrifts was a key to economic prosperity and that the state should intervene to ensure a sufficient level of activity.[11] Thus the Keynesian position predates the so-called classical tradition identified with Say's law of markets.

The first dispute between Keynes and Hayek, at the beginning of the 1930s, ended inconclusively. Then, after the publication of *The General Theory,* Keynes's victory was total. But the winds appear to be shifting again. We now witness a revival of the Turgot-Smith position, in a new guise. This is why it is justifiably referred to as 'new classical'. It is also the revenge of Hayek and his disciples. As for the future course of events, we can conclude with a message derived from both Keynes and Hayek. There is no way to predict with any kind of certainty. We can only choose a path, according to our moral and political convictions, without being sure of where it will lead us.

Notes

1.   We acknowledge the assistance of the Social Sciences and Humanities Research Council of Canada. Professor Samuel Bostaph, of the University of Dallas, read the first version of this text at the History of Economics meeting. We are grateful for his comments which helped us in the revision. We are also grateful to Venant Cauchy, of Montreal University, and Marguerite Mendell, of Concordia University, for their generous help with the English version of this text, first written in French. We are solely responsible for the remaining imperfections and mistakes.

2.   Keynes's *Treatise on Probability,* published in 1921, was written between 1906 and 1914. The first draft of Hayek's *The Sensory Order,* published in 1952, was written at the beginning of the twenties. On Hayek, see G. Dostaler and D. Ethier (1989).

3.   This text, read by Keynes to the Bloomsbury Memoir Club in 1938, is reprinted in *The Collected Writings of John Maynard Keynes,* London, Macmillan, Volume X, pp. 433–50. From now on, this edition of Keynes's work will be referred to as JMK, followed by the volume number.

4.   Compare, for example, Keynes's *Quarterly Journal of Economics* article with Hayek's 'Economics and Knowledge', published the same year (1937c).

5.   'Son écroulement définitif [of "the policy of the desperado", as Hayek called Keynesian policies, G.D.] était cependant inévitable, précisément pour les raisons exposées systématiquement, pour la première fois, dans ce petit livre.... Il se peut que l'effondrement de l'illusion keynésienne auquel on est en train d'assister donne à l'autre explication des

causes du chômage présentée dans ce livre davantage de chances d'être écoutée qu'il y a quarante ans' (Hayek, 1975, pp. 55–6).

6. See the testimony of A. Brown (1988). Among the comparisons between the two theories published at that time, see A.H. Hansen and H. Tout (1933), G.L.S. Shackle (1933) and J. Tinbergen (1935).
7. See also Hawtrey's review of *Monetary Theory and the Trade Cycle* (1933).
8. Many of these articles are reproduced in Hayek (1939) and Hayek (1984).
9. Published while we were completing this text.
10. We must underscore the criticisms of N. Kaldor, a former 'Hayekian' who was now as virulently anti-Hayek as Sraffa ten years ealier (Kaldor, 1942). See also R.G. Hawtrey (1941), L.M. Lachmann (1940), F.A. Lutz (1943), A.C. Pigou (1941), H. Townshend (1940), and T. Wilson (1940).
11. On this, see the exhaustive and scholarly account of Hutchison (1988).

References

Brown, A. (1988), 'A Worm's Eye View of the Keynesian Revolution', in J. Hillard (ed.), *J.M. Keynes in Retrospect: The Legacy of the Keynesian Revolution*, Aldershot: Edward Elgar, pp. 18–44.

Dostaler, G. and Ethier, D. (eds) (1989), *Friedrich Hayek: Philosophie, économie et politique*, Paris: Economica.

Graham, F.D. (1944), 'Keynes vs. Hayek on a Commodity Reserve Currency', *Economic Journal*, **54**, pp. 422–9.

Hansen, A.H. and Tout, H. (1933), 'Annual Survey of Business Cycle Theory: Investment and Saving in Business Cycle Theory', *Econometrica*, **1**, pp. 119–47.

Hawtrey, R.G. (1932), '*Prices and Production*. by F.A. Hayek', *Economica*, **12**, pp. 119–25.

Hawtrey, R.G. (1933), '*Monetary Theory and the Trade Cycle*. by F.A. Hayek', *Economic Journal*, **43**, pp. 669–72.

Hawtrey, R.G. (1941), 'Professor Hayek's Pure Theory of Capital', *Economic Journal*, **51**, pp. 281–90.

Hayek, F.A. (1925), 'The Monetary Policy of the United States after the Recovery from the 1920 Crisis', *Zeitschrift für Volkswirtschaft und Sozialpolitik*, n.s., **5**; partly reprinted in Hayek (1984), pp. 5–33.

Hayek, F.A. (1928), 'Intertemporal Price Equilibrium and Movements in the Value of Money', *Weltwirtschaftliches Archiv*, **28**, pp. 33–76; in Hayek (1984), pp. 71–117.

Hayek, F.A. (1931a), *Prices and Production*, London: Routledge & Son; (1932), New York: Macmillan.

Hayek, F.A. (1931b), 'Reflections on the Pure Theory of Money of Mr. J.M. Keynes', *Economica*, **11**, pp. 270–95.

Hayek, F.A. (1931c), 'A Rejoinder to Mr Keynes', *Economica*, **11**, pp. 398–403.

Hayek, F.A. (1931d), 'The "Paradox" of Saving', *Economica*, **11**, pp. 125–69.

Hayek, F.A. (1932a), 'Reflections on the Pure Theory of Money of Mr. J.M. Keynes (*continued*)', *Economica*, **12**, pp. 22–44.

Hayek, F.A. (1932b), 'Money and Capital: A Reply', *Economic Journal*, **42**, pp. 237–49.

Hayek, F.A. (1932c), '*Trade Depression and the Way Out*. by R.G. Hawtrey', *Economica*, **12**, pp. 126–7.

Hayek, F.A. (1933), *Monetary Theory and the Trade Cycle*, transl. N. Kaldor and H.M. Croome, London: Jonathan Cape; New York: Harcourt Brace; reprint, (1966), New York: Augustus M. Kelley.

Hayek, F.A. (1936), 'Utility Analysis and Interest', *Economic Journal*, **46**, pp. 44–60.

Hayek, F.A. (1937a), *Monetary Nationalism and International Stability*, London: Longmans, Green and Co.

Hayek, F.A. (1937b), 'Investment that Raises the Demand for Capital', *Review of Economic Statistics*, **19**, pp. 174–7; in Hayek (1939), pp. 73–82.

Hayek, F.A. (1937c), 'Economics and Knowledge', *Economica*, n.s., **4**, pp. 33–54.

Hayek, F.A. (1939), *Profits, Interest and Investment and Other Essays on The Theory of Industrial Fluctuations*, London: Routledge and Kegan Paul; reprint, (1969) New York: Augustus M. Kelley.

Hayek, F.A. (1941), *The Pure Theory of Capital*, London: Routledge & Kegan Paul; Chicago: University of Chicago Press.

Hayek, F.A. (1943), 'A Commodity Reserve Currency', *Economic Journal*, 53, pp. 176–84.

Hayek, F.A. (1944), *The Road to Serfdom*, London: George Routledge & Sons.

Hayek, F.A. (1952), *The Sensory Order: An Inquiry into the Foundations of Theoretical Psychology*, London: Routledge & Kegan Paul; Chicago: University of Chicago Press.

Hayek, F.A. (1975), *Prix et production*, transl. Tradecom, Paris: Calmann-Levy.

Hayek, F.A. (1978), *New Studies in Philosophy, Politics, Economics and the History of Ideas*, London: Routledge & Kegan Paul; Chicago: University of Chicago Press.

Hayek, F.A. (1984), *Money, Capital and Fluctuations: Early Essays*, ed. R. McCloughry, London: Routledge & Kegan Paul; Chicago: University of Chicago Press.

Hayek, F.A. (1988), *The Fatal Conceit*, vol. 1 of *The Collected Works of F.A. Hayek*, ed. W.W. Bartley III, London: Routledge; (1989) Chicago: University of Chicago Press.

Hicks, J.R. (1967), 'The Hayek Story', in *Critical Essays in Monetary Theory*, Oxford: Oxford University Press, pp. 203–15.

Hutchison, T.W. (1988), *Before Adam Smith: The Emergence of Political Economy 1662–1776*, Oxford: Basil Blackwell.

Kahn, R.F. (1984), *The Making of Keynes' General Theory*, Cambridge: Cambridge University Press.

Kaldor, N. (1942), 'Professor Hayek and the Concertina-Effect', *Economica*, n.s., 9, pp. 359–82.

Keynes, J.M. (1943), 'The Objective of International Price Stability', *Economic Journal*, 53, pp. 185–7.

Keynes, J.M. (1944), 'Note by Lord Keynes', *Economic Journal*, 54, pp. 429–30.

Keynes, J.M. (1971–1989), *The Collected Writings of John Maynard Keynes*, 30 volumes, London: Macmillan.

Lachmann, L.M. (1940), 'A Reconsideration of the Austrian Theory of Industrial Fluctuations', *Economica*, n.s., 7, pp. 179–96.

Lutz, F.A. (1943), 'Professor Hayek's Theory of Interest', *Economica*, n.s., 10, pp. 302–10.

Pigou, A.C. (1941), 'Maintaining Capital Intact, on F.A. von Hayek *The Pure Theory of Capital*', *Economica*, n.s., 8, pp. 271–75.

Robinson, J. (1933), 'A Parable on Savings and Investment', *Economica*, 13, pp. 75–84.

Shackle, G.L.S. (1933), 'Some Notes on Monetary Theories of the Trade Cycle', *Review of Economic Studies*, 1, pp. 27–38.

Sraffa, P. (1932), 'Dr Hayek on Money and Capital', *Economic Journal*, 42, pp. 42–53.

Tinbergen, J. (1935), 'Annual Survey: Suggestions on Quantitative Business Cycle Theory', *Econometrica*, 3, pp. 241–308.

Townshend, H. (1940), '*Profits, Interest and Investment* by F.A. von Hayek', *Economic Journal*, 50, pp. 99–103.

Wilson, T. (1940), 'Capital Theory and the Trade Cycle', *Review of Economic Studies*, pp. 169–79.

7   Hutt and Keynes

Leland B. Yeager

William H. Hutt's career involved work on three continents. Born in London in 1899, he studied at the London School of Economics. From 1928 to 1965, the University of Cape Town in South Africa was his academic base. He subsequently emigrated to the United States, teaching at several American universities. He died in 1988.

Hutt was a wide-ranging scholar. Like John Maynard Keynes, he contributed to topics beyond monetary theory and macroeconomics (see, for example, Reynolds, 1986). In *Economists and the Public* and *Politically Impossible...?* he waxed philosophical, exploring the proper role of academic economists in debates over public policy. He counselled academics to cherish their ivory-tower purity, avoiding even the appearance of speaking for political parties or industries or other private interests, in order to preserve their scientific authority. They should not compromise in hope of being influential. Hutt was '"sufficient of a realist to know that the chances of . . . exercising any influence on policy are small". Every true economist in this age must be satisfied with great hopes and small expectations' (1952a, p. 53, quoting the preface to his own *Theory of Idle Resources*). When an economist does consider *political* feasibility and so recommends a policy other than the one he considers best on grounds of economics (and avowable value judgements), then he should clearly state the amateur political assessment underlying his recommendation, and also state the policy he truly considers best. Keynes, unlike Hutt, relished active involvement outside academia. He wrote much on policy issues, was confident of his ability to sway public opinion first one way and then another (as he mentioned in a conversation recalled by F.A. Hayek, 1979, pp. 101–2), and was inclined to develop theory to bolster existing policy intuitions. As its title suggests, however, this chapter concentrates on work for which Hutt and Keynes are best known and in which they treat the same topics – their money-macro theories.

Keynes on demand failure

As the *General Theory* in particular shows, Keynes believed in a deep-seated, recurrent tendency toward deficiency of effective demand, causing unemployment and loss of potential output. Keynes had no particular complaint about how the price mechanism would allocate resources, given adequate total demand. Especially in wealthy communities, however, private investment tended to be inadequate to absorb all the saving that would be attempted at full employment. Although Keynes and his followers sometimes identified the difficulty as characteristic of a monetary economy as opposed to a barter economy, they did not trace deficiency of demand to an unstable and often wrong quantity of money. Even though Keynes waffled a bit on the question of monetary disorder (notably in Chapter 17 of the *General Theory*), he definitely was not a monetarist in today's sense of the word. Monetary disequilibrium, if it occurred, reflected *real* troubles; he saw market failure, particularly failures centred in the labour and stock and bond markets. He believed that on average over time, business investment was inadequate for full employment and was prone to fluctuate with the state of business confidence, which in turn was subject to sudden change because estimates of prospective yield had to be made using limited knowledge. Keynes alluded to waves of optimism and pessimism, an antisocial fetish of liquidity, and 'dark forces of time and ignorance' enveloping the future (1936, pp. 153–5). For such reasons, he thought that an acceptable approximation to full employment required sustained government action to maintain adequate total spending. (To avoid repeating myself in detail, and for documentation, I refer to my 1986b.)

Hutt's micro orientation

Hutt's macroeconomics is more disaggregative and micro-oriented. Hutt adopts a Say's Law, or goods-against-goods, approach. People specialize in producing particular goods and services to trade them away for the specialized outputs of other people. Incomes created in particular lines of production are the sources of demand for the outputs of other lines: supply of some things constitutes demand for other (non-competing) things. Fundamentally, then, there can be no deficiency of demand. Any apparent problem of that sort traces to impediments to the exchange of goods and services for each other. Impediments to exchange discourage the production of goods and services destined for exchange and discourage the employment of labour and other productive factors. Diagnosing these impediments is Hutt's overriding concern.

Say's Law, as Hutt interprets and extends it, explains how cuts in production in some sectors of the economy entail cuts in real demands for the outputs of other sectors and so cuts in production in those other sectors also. The rot is cumulative; disequilibrium is infectious; a multiplier process operates, although not in the mechanistic way suggested by Keynes's spuriously precise formulas. In the opposite and more cheerful direction, anything promoting recovery of production in some sectors promotes recovery in other sectors also.

But what are the impediments to exchange and production that trigger the downward movement and whose alleviation triggers cumulative recovery? Hutt points to wrong prices. Prices too high to clear the markets for the outputs of some sectors cause cutbacks in their production and in their demands for the outputs of other sectors. What might otherwise have been equilibrium prices for the outputs of those other sectors are now too high; and unless adjusted downwards, they impede exchanges and production further. Hutt blames wrong pricing, not any inadequacy of 'spending'. Instead of determining the volume of exchanges, spending gets determined: the flow of money transferred in lubricating transactions depends on their physical volume and on the money prices at which those real transactions are evaluated. It is fallacious to suppose, with the Keynesians, that income is created by transfers of money (Hutt, 1979, pp. 90, 381). Hutt does not flatly assert that monetary disorder never plays any role at all in frustrating exchanges and production. His view of the role of money will require further attention later in this chapter. Meanwhile, we may note his remark that 'Money is relevant to "effective demand" only because *unanticipated* inflation can, in a very crude way, cause certain prices which have been forced above market-clearing levels (causing therefore nonuse or underuse of men and assets) to become market-clearing values, thereby releasing "withheld" potential productive capacity and increasing "effective demand" in our sense *and* in Keynes' sense' (Hutt, 1977, p. 36, emphasis in original).

Hutt scorns the fundamentalist Keynesianism that broods about adequacy or inadequacy of demand, about the propensity to consume out of real income, and about a savings gap that grows with income and wealth and so supposedly becomes all the harder to fill with real investment spending, especially as real capital formation supposedly leaves fewer and fewer attractive opportunities for still further investment. Saving, as such, cannot pose a problem. People cannot save without acquiring some assets or other. If this process, including the associated financial transactions, results in real capital formation, well and good; opportunities for further investment still are not foreclosed. Complementarities exist among capital goods; having more of some expands profitable opportunities to construct more of others. Furthermore, sectors of the economy employing additional capital goods enjoy increased productivity and real incomes, which increase the demands for the outputs of other sectors and for the resources to produce them. If, on the other hand, savers neither acquire real assets themselves nor acquire securities by transferring their command over resources to entrepreneurs who will construct assets, then they must be trying to build up their holdings of money. Yet Keynes, says Hutt, tried to put the blame on an excessive propensity to save as such, obscuring the liquidity-preference or demand-for-money aspect of the disequilibrium. (This charge, it seems to me, overlooks chapter 17 of the *General Theory*. What Keynes might better be charged with is vagueness, along with inconsistency among different parts of his book.)

Actually, says Hutt (1979, p. 295), 'saving preference and liquidity preference are as unrelated as demands for monocles and bubble gum'. Even when
an intensified demand for money balances is contributing to macroeconomic
disequilibrium, the blame should fall not on this particular change in preferences
but on the failure of prices to accommodate it. With prices insufficiently
flexible, *any* change in technology or resources or preferences, including not
only a strengthening but even a weakening of savings preference or of liquidity
preference, can impede market-clearing, exchanges, and production. Diagnosis
must thus focus on how well or poorly the pricing process is working, and why.

Disequilibrium theories
In emphasizing the infectiousness of the failure of some markets to clear (and,
more cheerfully, the cumulative character of recovery when some prices
initiate adjustment to market-clearing levels), Hutt's doctrine parallels a line of
advance in macroeconomics pioneered by Robert Clower (1965, 1967) and
Axel Leijonhufvud (1968) and followed by such other economists as Donald
Tucker (1971) and Robert Barro and Herschel Grossman (1971, 1976). Their
approach features such concepts as absence of the (supposed) Walrasian
auctioneer, incomplete and costly and imperfect information, false price
signals, sluggish price adjustments, quantity changes as well as price adjustments, the duality of people's decisions about particular transactions according
to whether they do or do not meet frustration in accomplishing other desired
transactions, and the income-constrained process (the counterpart of Hutt's
infectiousness of disequilibrium and recovery).

Clower and Leijonhufvud offered their approach as spelling out what
Keynes 'really meant' or 'had at the back of his mind' while writing the *General
Theory*. In this they were wrong, in my opinion. Actually, they were independently resurrecting an older approach from which the Keynesian revolution
had diverted attention (Yeager, 1973; cf. Grossman, 1972). Hutt believes that
his own remarkably similar doctrine stands poles apart from what he considers
the crudities of Keynes. (In a thesis on *Theories of Disequilibrium: Clower and
Leijonhufvud Compared to Hutt*, Mrs. Evelyn Marr Glazier notes but does not
actually tackle the question of who more correctly understands what Keynes
really meant. She does, however, show that the three economists named in her
title 'agree more on some of the fundamental issues of disequilibrium than they
do on the history of doctrines' (p. 3).)

Hutt differs from Clower and Leijonhufvud more in emphasis than on
substance. He puts less emphasis than they do on reasons why a considerable
degree of price and wage stickiness is understandable and rational. He does not
recognize why, after a disturbance, it naturally takes time to achieve a new
equilibrium level and co-ordinated pattern of prices because of incompleteness
and costliness of and delays in obtaining up-to-date knowledge of market

conditions and the interdependence yet separate and sequential setting and revision of individual prices and wages. (On this latter point, see Cagan, 1980 and Yeager, 1986a.)

Hutt notes that Clower and Leijonhufvud stress 'the imperfections of the information and communication process as a cause of the *hiatus*' that money poses between desires to sell and desires to buy.

> But the kind of communication or information required for the coordination of the economy takes the form of market pressures; and these pressures are exerted through loss-avoidance, profit-seeking incentives. Faced with such market signals as shrinking or accumulating inventories, entrepreneurs react by changing the rates of liquidation of different inventories via the price changes which they forecast will effect the desired results (Hutt, 1974, p. 102, emphasis in original).

Market processes thwarted

In passages where he seems about to recognize the natural aspect of price and wage stickiness (for example, 1974, pp. 40–41), Hutt does not follow through. He regrets the less than instantaneous operation of market pressures and returns to the theme that wrong prices in other economic sectors 'merely' make price cuts necessary for market-clearing in a particular sector (1974, pp. 40–41, 89–90). He notes that if an entrepreneur *correctly* expects a decline in demand for his product to prove temporary, then letting its inventory grow will turn out to have been a wise investment. If he proves wrong, then he will have withheld supplies, and his misbehaviour has depressive effects on other sectors. Market processes, however, including the natural selection of entrepreneurs, will generally achieve quick adjustment of prices to market-clearing levels if only they are allowed to work (1974, pp. 44–5, 97). Even if government policy aimed at preventing misbehaviour in the pricing process, it admittedly could not succeed completely. 'There would always be defects in the drafting of the required legislation, as well as error in enforcement and judicial interpretations' (1974, pp. 41–2). So saying, Hutt again blames imperfect policy rather than natural conditions. Entrepreneurial pessimism or timidity in depressions has always been 'a consequence of the price mechanism having been prevented from fulfilling its co-ordinative role' (1974, p. 99). Note the word 'prevented'.

Hutt blames government for not suppressing the basic reason – villainy – why prices and wages do not clear markets and assure continuous co-ordination. He perceives villainy – but the word is mine, not his – on the part of labour unions, business monopolists, and government itself. Villainy includes such things as union control over wages, minimum-wage laws, overgenerous unemployment compensation, and monopoly and collusion. Hutt recognizes that the victims of incorrect pricing are not necessarily the villains. Villainous pricing of particular factors and outputs can reduce the demands for other outputs, rendering their unchanged prices wrong and their producers idle (for example, Hutt, 1974, p. 88). However, he is inclined to criticize even these victims of others' malpricing for not adapting to the changed situation by adjusting their own prices promptly and steeply enough (1974, p. 83).

Throughout his many writings (for example, Hutt, 1973) Hutt denounces union wage scales and strikes. Even the mere possibility of strikes deters productive investment and so the growth of real incomes. Even for me, no great admirer of unions, his repeated fulminations against them become downright boring.

Hutt's book of 1944, containing proposals for post-war Britain in particular, further expounds his diagnosis by displaying his passion for reconstructing the world along idealized competitive lines. Drastic antitrust laws would prohibit strikes, lockouts, and boycotts; contracts or conspiracies to restrain output, trade, or exchange or to take part in collusive monopolies; price discrimination; amalgamations, mergers, and holding companies; acquisition by a corporation of shares or debentures of other corporations or purchase, as a going concern, of the assets of competitors; and interlocking directorates. A State Trading Board would have the right to compete with private enterprise, to expropriate property, to impose schemes for co-ordination, synchronization, and stand-ardization upon groups of independent firms, to determine hours and conditions of labour in certain circumstances, to certify quality, and to issue cease-and-desist orders. A Labour Security Board might require young people to accept specified training or apprenticeship and might penalize failure to attend regularly and perform with due diligence. A Resources Utilization Commission would require State corporations and owners of public utilities to practise marginal-cost pricing, unless aggregate receipts would be less than fixed cost plus avoidable cost. Hutt gave a definition of marginal cost and added: 'In the interpretation of this definition recourse may be had to the text-books of economics' (1944, quotation from p. 62).

I doubt that Hutt would still, late in his career, have advocated such drastic steps toward making reality conform to textbook chapters on pure and perfect competition. In the intervening years he, like so many of the rest of us, presumably learned much about the interrelations between economic freedom and human freedom in general; he presumably became disenchanted about turning to government for solutions to market failures. But his book of 1944 remains symptomatic of an orientation that Hutt apparently did hold throughout his career – a concern to trace macroeconomic difficulties to impediments to the ideal working of markets and to seek remedies through microeconomic re-constructions. In his book of 1974 (pp. 101–2) he still suggested that antitrust action, if not perverted by demagogic vote-seeking, would be an appropriate and important ingredient of policy for full employment. Pre-Keynesian economists whom he admired believed 'that unless government performed its classical role *there was an automatic tendency for groups acting in collusion to price their inputs or outputs in such a way that a cumulative tendency for economies to run down could be set in motion'* (1974, p. 120, emphasis Hutt's).

Hutt and the Clower–Leijonhufvud school differ, as we have seen, in their relative emphases on villainy and reasonable behaviour in explaining wage and price stickiness. (I do not want to suggest, however, that the latter school stresses rigidity or even stickiness as the ultimate source of discoordination. Clower and Leijonhufvud probe more deeply into the intricate and prolonged groping necessary to enlist scattered knowledge and achieve a new market-clearing level and pattern of prices after a major shock. On this distinction, see, in particular, Leijonhufvud, 1981, pp. 111–12.)

Hutt on money
Another point on which emphases differ concerns the role of money in economic discoordination. Clower in particular (for example, 1967) emphasizes that goods do not exchange for goods *directly*: money is the medium of exchange, and if people have difficulty obtaining money by selling their own goods or services, that very fact keeps them from expressing their demands for other people's goods and services.

Hutt is sceptical of this notion of money as a hiatus between selling and buying.

> [W]hen a person buys, he normally demands with *money's worth*, not with money. He demands with money only when he happens to be reducing his investment in it (i.e., not concurrently replenishing his money holdings), *for he can always obtain money costlessly by realizing his inputs or outputs (services or assets) as their money's worth. ... [T]he acquisition and spending of money ... is costless.* It follows that money is as incidental (and as important) as cash registers and cashiers in the demanding and supplying process (Hutt, 1974, pp. 67–8, emphasis Hutt's; cf. pp. 57–60).

In this passage Hutt seems to be supposing a unified budget constraint, in contrast with the realistic split constraint described by Clower (1967). He also seems to suppose that all goods and services are extremely liquid or readily marketable at their full values. His downplaying of the role of money as medium of exchange may be associated with his defining the quantity of money very broadly so as to include what he calls the 'pure money equivalent' of nearmoneys and nonmoneys (Hutt, 1974, pp. 17–18, and 1979, chapter 8).

The possible frustration of transactions through failure of communications and market signals does not basically trace to the use of money. The hiatus arises from the remoteness of wage-earner and wage-earner, of entrepreneur and entrepreneur. These remotenesses are inevitable consequences of the extreme division of labour that the pricing system and money make possible. Except in this sense, the use of money has nothing whatever to do with the problem. (These sentences closely paraphrase 1974, pp. 58–9.)

Yet one would expect someone who expounds the tremendous services of money as eloquently as Hutt does (for example, 1974, p. 60) to recognize the correspondingly great scope for damage if the real quantity of money comes to deviate seriously from the total of real cash balances demanded. One would expect that recognition from the author of 'The Yield on Money Held' (1956), an absolutely fundamental contribution to monetary theory. (Hutt explains the straightforward senses in which business cash balances are productive and consumers' cash balances afford utility. A brilliant exposition and extension by Selgin, 1987, makes further discussion here unnecessary.)

Yet Hutt says he does not understand why the tastes, market processes, and so forth that determine the purchasing power of the money unit should induce 'income constraints in the form of the withholding of supplies and hence of demands, except in the sense that, in the presence of downward cost and price rigidities, deflation will aggravate the cumulative withholding process – just as *unanticipated* inflation will mitigate or reverse it' (1974, p. 62, emphasis in original). Whether Hutt realizes it or not, the exception he makes is a mammoth one. He also appears to recognize the damage that an inappropriate quantity of money can do when he quotes Leijonhufvud, with apparent agreement, concerning 'recurrent attacks of central bank perversity' (1974, p. 73, quoting Leijonhufvud, 1968, p. 399, where, however, Leijonhufvud capitalizes the initial letters of 'Central Bank'.)

Yet Hutt shies away from recognizing the role of money in business cycles and from appreciating the monetary-disequilibrium hypothesis of David Hume, Clark Warburton, Milton Friedman, Karl Brunner, Allan Meltzer, and other monetarists. In an oblique reference to the monetary aspect of depression, Hutt did go so far as to say that the classical orthodoxy of the 1920s and 1930s had warned against 'the development of an inflationary situation which, requiring subsequent deflationary ratification *if contractual monetary obligations were to be honored*, would eventually precipitate depression through predictable resistances to the necessary price adjustments' (Hutt, 1974, p. 118, emphasis in original). In several places, furthermore, Hutt appears to advocate a policy of accommodating the quantity of money to the demand to hold it at a stable price level.

Even so, he backs away from tracing macroeconomic disorder to money. When he comes as close as he ever does to comparing monetary disturbances and price rigidities as sources of disruption, he almost always puts his emphasis on the rigidities (for example, 1974, p. 69). The nonmonetary view of depression, he says, 'is truly the explanation of *all* depression. When deflation is the initiating factor (under downward cost or price rigidity), the economy still runs through the cumulative consequences of the withdrawal of supplies of non-money' (1974, p. 73n, emphasis in original).

[D]epression is due to the chronic, continuous boosting of costs in occupations and industries where the unions tend to be strongest – because demands for their outputs happen to be most inelastic and consumers therefore most easily exploited. In the absence of inflation it would have been perceived how the withdrawal of labour and output by over-pricing in such activities reduces the source of demands for the outputs of less easily exploitable occupations and activities (1975, p. 113, footnotes omitted here).

But one might well expect Hutt to explain why a 'chronic' and 'continuous' problem manifests itself in only occasional depressions, with healthy growth and occasional booms intervening. Later Hutt says that inflation, if unanticipated, can improve price/cost ratios in many sectors of the economy. But this crude remedy attracts resources into unsustainable kinds of production and 'creates such basic distortions in the pricing mechanism that *we must often blame the attempt to spend depression into prosperity for aggravating prospective and realised unemployment*' (1975, pp. 113–14, emphasis in original).

Hutt touches on certain crucial questions about money without giving sufficiently explicit answers. In some passages he takes such pains to penetrate behind the veil of money that he practically denies money's routine but momentously important function as the medium of exchange; he actually says that people are buying goods and services with money only when, untypically, they are acting to reduce their cash balances (1979, pp. 238, 295). When inflation appears to be stimulating a depressed economy – a phenomenon supposedly beloved of the Keynesians – does the stimulus come from the monetary expansion as such, with prices lagging and the quantity of money and flow of spending thus growing in real terms, or from the price inflation itself, which may be rectifying wrong relative prices, especially by eroding excessively high real wage rates? Often Hutt appears to give the latter answer, suggesting that the trick of getting real wages down in a relatively politically feasible way is the essence of Keynesian employment policy. Interpreters disagree, but others have also taken Keynes to mean just that. It would be ironic if Hutt and Keynes, when agreeing, agree on an erroneous point.

In a malcoordinated and depressed economy, does the trouble necessarily stem from wrong *relative* prices, such as excessive real wages, or might it stem instead mainly from prices and wages that, although not badly out of line with one another, are *generally* too high (or conceivably too low) in relation to the nominal quantity of money? In some passages (September 1953, p. 224; 1979, pp. 147, 282–3, and *passim*) Hutt emphasizes *unstable* price rigidities and people's postponement of purchases while waiting for the rigidities to break down and prices to fall, seeming to imply that the particular price level would not matter if its *permanent* rigidity were obviating these expectations and postponements. In other passages (1979, pp. 185–6, 207, and *passim*) he seems to advocate a policy of flexibly accommodating the nominal quantity of money to the existing price level, as if he were indeed concerned about the painful necessity of otherwise adjusting the price and wage level to the money supply.

Hutt anticipated some of the soundest parts of the present-day doctrine of rational expectations. He emphasizes that when inflation has come to be generally expected and allowed for, it becomes purposeless. Unemployment becomes almost a normal accompaniment of inflation, even accelerating inflation (1977, pp.37–8; cf. p. 252). In these and other passages, however, it is unclear whether he sees the underlying money-supply expansion itself or instead sees the resulting price inflation as what may initially stimulate or recoordinate an economy (although eventually becoming futile). Apparently he means the latter: price inflation may be a way – an inferior, temporary, Keynesian way – of improving co-ordination by inflating down excessively high real wage rates. He does not forthrightly grapple with the monetarist point that depression may occur not so much because *relative* prices and wages are wrong as because the whole wage and price level is too high in relation to the nominal quantity of money or, in other words, because the nominal money supply has become too small for the wage and price level.

Hutt's style of argument
Readers must wish that Hutt had done what he did not do, namely systematically present the doctrines he considered rivals of his own in their strongest versions, criticize them in adequate detail, and show just how they fail where his succeeds. We know Hutt disliked Keynesianism; it would be interesting to know in some detail what he thought about monetarist reasoning and evidence.

Hutt's failure to make his position clear on crucial issues, together with the writing style that is largely responsible, brings to mind his own complaint (for example, in 1979, Prologue) about how little scholarly dialogue his work had elicited, particularly from Keynesians. (Consider, also, the harsh review of Hutt 1974 by Herschel Grosman, 1976, someone who I think would be sympathetic to much of Hutt's message if it were presented clearly.)

Hutt's exposition is a collection of discursive and often cryptic remarks. Strewn over hundreds of pages (in 1979, for example), and in no readily intelligible order, we find bits of positive analysis, jabs at Keynesianism, historical allusions, policy proposals, and autobiographical asides. Hutt had a habit of latching onto remarks by other writers as they were apparently cast up at random by his own reading, even if those writers were not leading or typical authorities or controversialists on the points at issue, and then using their remarks as pegs onto which to string his own observations. This habit gave his writing an unnecessarily polemical tone. (As Pejovich, 1978, noted, Hutt had a normative bent and seemed not particularly concerned with non-normative analysis of allocations generated by alternative institutional arrangements.)

Strewn through Hutt's writings are echoes of long-standing obsessions, including, of course, his obsession with labour unions. Another concerns Britain's return to the gold standard in 1925 at the pre-war parity, requiring internal deflation if that parity were to remain workable. Repeatedly, though often in cryptic language, Hutt offered apologetics for that policy. He might even have been right, but the way that these apologetics kept intruding in unlikely places and with a moralizing tone is characteristic of his style.

Another characteristic is lengthy brooding over the meanings of terms and concepts. Hutt once recorded his 'strong dislike for mere "terminological innovation"' (September 1953, p. 215), but this is a dislike that he managed to overcome. Some wag once said that he wrote in Huttite. Hutt offered lengthy and sometimes obscure definitions of such concepts as market-clearing prices for inputs (1977, p. 105), competition (1977, p. 154; 1974, pp. 15–16), exploitation (1977, p. 218n.), money (1977, p. 254), and some nine or ten varieties of idleness (throughout his 1977). Presumably out of aversion to theorizing with aggregates and averages, Hutt avoided the term 'price level', saying 'scale of prices' instead (for example, September 1953, p. 217; 1979, p. 214).

Hutt used one term so much that I, anyway, became accustomed to it: 'withheld capacity'. This term suggests that people who, in ordinary language, are having a hard time finding jobs or customers are *withholding* their capacity to work or produce by insisting on wages or prices above market-clearing levels. So doing, they are withholding their demands for the goods and services of other people and thereby causing other prices and wages, if unchanged, to be excessive. This terminological allusion to villainy serves to shunt aside analysis of the nature and reasons for price and wage stickiness, including ways that the interdependence of wages and prices narrows the reasonable options available to individual price-setters and wage negotiators. His terminology helps Hutt to damn reality for being real. Yet he himself briefly recognized (for example, 1977, pp. 136n., 204) that resistance to wage and price adjustments can be 'individually rational' although 'collectively irrational'.

His terminology would permit him, if pressed, to defend propositions that are startling on their face.

1. The withholding of capacity which is capable of providing currently valuable services is always a case of restraint on freedom (1979, p. 371n.).

2. [T]he labor of all able-bodied persons was demanded throughout the depression years. *It was not supplied* (1979, p. 169).

3. [W]hat is usually called 'unemployed labor' could be more realistically called 'unsupplied labor' (1974, p. 79).

4. Individuals actively 'prospecting' for remunerative jobs are employed (italicized section heading in 1977, p. 83).

5. [In the] phrase 'excess supply' of labor ... the word 'excess' ... could more appropriately be 'deficient' or 'insufficient'! (1974, p. 86).

6. [T]he phrase 'willingness to demand' ... simply means 'willingness to supply'! (1974, p. 27).

7. [W]hen there is a 'shortage' or rationing, we usually say that 'demand exceeds supply', although what we really mean is that, at the price asked, more *would* be demanded if more were supplied. Hence I cannot conceive of any situation in which ... the value and amount demanded in any market fails to equal the value and amount supplied. ... [P]eople who *would be* prepared to demand at the price asked if they could get the goods are prevented from demanding (1974, pp. 80–81).

8. [C]onsumption is always the *extermination* of power to demand. The failure of the Keynesians to understand this simple truth lies at the root of what I believe to be the most outrageous intellectual error of this age (1979, p. 341).

Hutt often covered himself against challenge by qualifying apparently egregious propositions with cryptic phrases that are hardly understandable unless the reader is already familiar with his terminology and allusions. For example,

> It is quite wrong to assume that unfavorable prospects can deter net accumulations, otherwise than through the discouragement of saving preference, or – indirectly – through the encouragement of the withholding of capacity (although such prospects certainly do influence the *form* taken by accumulation) (1979, p. 349).

A similar habit was to mention government policies not always straightforwardly but rather with reference to the results that Hutt would expect them to have. Thus, in an historical context: 'not a single governmental step toward multiplying the wages flow was taken' (italicized in 1979, p. 61), meaning, approximately, that the government did not act against the unions.

The selling of ideas
Besides his terminology, tone, and paradox-mongering, other circumstances help explain why Hutt's work has received less attention than Keynes's. Although the *General Theory* was not Keynes's best-written book, it does contain flashes of clever writing and appealing new concepts and terminology. Keynes presented his message as revolutionary, offering young or adaptable economists the opportunity to march at the vanguard of the profession. Keynes's theory had political appeal. It came as a rationalization (whether sound or unsound) of policies that would have been beneficial under the exceptional circumstances of the mid-1930s. Hutt, though, was recommending micro-oriented policies that would have stepped on toes and whose desired benefits would not have come quickly.

Hutt always maintained that he was expounding old, orthodox doctrine; but, although alluding to Edwin Cannan and the London School tradition, he did not build on his predecessors' work in adequate detail, and he neglected to forge links with pre-Keynesian monetary-disequilibrium theory. So he put himself at a double-barreled disadvantage – confessing that his message was basically old stuff, while not clearly showing how he was extending it. Keynes's theory, in contrast, appealed to academic economists by containing concepts and gimmicks offering possibilities for research and publication, for class lectures and examination questions. (On this matter of the internal dynamic of a field of study, see Colander, 1986.)

The enduring value of Hutt's message

Although I do think that Hutt created unnecessary difficulties for its acceptance, I do not mean to disparage his message itself. Apparent macro disorders can indeed trace partly to micro distortions, particularly in prices and wages. Because market transactions are voluntary and the short side determines the actual quantity traded in any market, frustration of transactions and so of production can cumulate in a quasi-multiplier process. Downward cumulativeness is particularly severe if money and credit undergo an induced or secondary deflation (although I do wish that Hutt had been more emphatic in recognizing the role of money). Like F.A. Hayek and others, Hutt was magnificently right in his strictures against chronically inflationary policies as supposed cures of unemployment.

Because of Hutt's style and tone, his writings are unlikely to persuade readers who lack the background and the will necessary to understand his eccentrically phrased message. (For two reasons I myself have been turned off by Hutt's style less than most readers probably would be. First, when I came across Hutt's work decades ago, I happened to be predisposed in favour of the sort of message he was trying to convey. Second, I was privileged in 1955 to attend a two-week conference at which he was one of the main speakers. Later, when he served as visiting professor at the University of Virginia, we were colleagues. His analytical message, his humanitarian concern for those suffering from restrictions on economic opportunity, his intellectual force and zeal, and his integrity came across better when he had ample opportunity to present his message in person than when he offered it in writing alone.)

Whether he realized it or not, Hutt was preaching to the already saved. Doing so, however, is far from pointless. Sympathetic readers can find much in his work to fortify their understanding of how the real world works and could be made to work better. They can find much to deepen their insights into the fallacies of Keynesian doctrines whose former dominance has still not been entirely expunged. Teachers able to give sympathetic expositions can make good use of Hutt's work in their classes. It may serve as the focus of fruitful controversy among sympathetic readers.

References

Barro, R.J. and Grossman, H.I. (1971), 'A General Disequilibrium Model of Income and Employment', *American Economic Review* **61**, (March), pp. 82–93.

Barro, R.J. and Grossman, H.I. (1976), *Money, Employment, and Inflation*, New York: Cambridge University Press.

Cagan, P. (1980), 'Reflections on Rational Expectations', *Journal of Money, Credit, and Banking*, **12**, (November), Part 2, pp. 826–32.

Clower, R.W. (1965), 'The Keynesian Counterrevolution: A Theoretical Appraisal', in F.H. Hahn and F.P.R. Brechling (eds), *The Theory of Interest Rates*, London: Macmillan, pp. 103–125.

Clower, R.W. (1967), 'A Reconsideration of the Microfoundations of Monetary Theory', *Western Economic Journal*, **6**, (December), pp. 1–8.

Colander, D.C. (1986), 'The Evolution of Keynesian Economics', unpublished manuscript dated 14 October 1986, prepared for presentation at Glendon College, York University, Conference on Keynes and Public Policy after Fifty Years.

Friedman, M. and Schwartz, A.J. (1963), *A Monetary History of the United States, 1867–1960*, Princeton: Princeton University Press.

Glazier, E.M. (1970), *Theories of Disequilibrium: Clower and Leijonhufvud Compared to Hutt*, Master's Thesis, University of Virginia.

Grossman, H.I. (1972), 'Was Keynes a "Keynesian"?' *Journal of Economic Literature*, **10**, pp. 26–30.

Grossman, H.I. (1976), Review of W.H. Hutt, *A Rehabilitation of Say's Law*, *The Manchester School of Economic and Social Studies*, **44**, (June), pp. 196–7.

Hayek, F.A. (1979), *A Tiger by the Tail*, San Francisco: Cato Institute.

Hutt, W.H. (1936), *Economists and the Public*, London: Jonathan Cape.

Hutt, W.H. (1944), *Plan for Reconstruction*, New York: Oxford University Press.

Hutt, W.H. (1952a), 'The Nature of Money', *South African Journal of Economics*, **20**, (March), pp. 50–64.

Hutt, W.H. (1952b), 'The Notion of the Volume of Money', *South African Journal of Economics*, **20**, (September), (mimeographed copy in lieu of a reprint).

Hutt, W.H. (1953), 'The Notion of Money of Constant Value', parts I and II, *South African Journal of Economics*, **21**, (September), pp. 215–26, and (December), pp. 341–53.

Hutt, W.H. (1954), 'The Significance of Price Flexibility', *South African Journal of Economics*, **22**, (March), pp. 40–51.

Hutt, W.H. (1956), 'The Yield from Money Held', in M. Sennholz, (ed.) *On Freedom and Free Enterprise*, pp. 196–216, Princeton: Van Nostrand.

Hutt, W.H. (1963), *Keynesianism – Retrospect and Prospect*, Chicago: Regnery.

Hutt, W.H. (1971), *Politically Impossible ...?* Hobart Paperback, London: Institute of Economic Affairs.

Hutt, W.H. (1973), *The Strike-Threat System*, New Rochelle: Arlington House.

Hutt, W.H. (1974), *A Rehabilitation of Say's Law*, Athens: Ohio University Press.

Hutt, W.H. (1975), *The Theory of Collective Bargaining, 1930–1975*, Hobart Paperback, London: Institute of Economic Affairs, second impression 1977 (first ed. 1930).

Hutt, W.H. (1977), *The Theory of Idle Resources: A Study in Definition*, Second ed. Indianapolis: Liberty Press, (first ed. 1939).

Hutt, W.H. (1979), *The Keynesian Episode: A Reassessment*, Indianapolis: Liberty Press.

Keynes, J.M. (1936), *The General Theory of Employment, Interest and Money*, New York: Harcourt, Brace.

Leijonhufvud, A. (1968), *On Keynesian Economics and the Economics of Keynes*, New York: Oxford University Press.

Leijonhufvud, A. (1981), *Information and Coordination*, New York: Oxford University Press.

Pejovich, S. (1978), Review of Armen Alchian, *Economic Forces at Work* and W.H. Hutt, *The Theory of Idle Resources*, *Modern Age*, **22**, (Winter), pp. 92–4.

Reynolds, M.O. (ed.) (1986), *W.H. Hutt: An Economist for the Long Run*, Chicago and Washington: Gateway Editions.

Selgin, G.A. (1987), 'The Yield on Money Held Revisited: Lessons for Today', *Market Process* (George Mason University), **5**, (1) Spring, pp. 18–24.

Tucker, D.P. (1971), 'Macroeconomic Models and the Demand for Money under Market Disequilibrium', *Journal of Money, Credit, and Banking*, **3**, (February), pp. 57–83.

Warburton, C. (1966), *Depression, Inflation, and Monetary Policy*, Baltimore: Johns Hopkins Press.

Warburton, C. (1981), 'Monetary Disequilibrium Theory in the First Half of the Twentieth Century', *History of Political Economy*, **13**, (Summer) pp. 285–99.

Yeager, L.B. (1973), 'The Keynesian Diversion', *Western Economic Journal* **11**, (June), pp. 150–63.

Yeager, L.B. (1986a), 'The Significance of Monetary Disequilibrium', *Cato Journal* **6**, (Fall), pp. 369–99.

Yeager, L.B. (1986b), 'The Keynesian Heritage in Economics', in John Burton and others, *Keynes's* General Theory: *Fifty Years On*, pp. 27–44, Hobart Paperback, London: Institute of Economic Affairs, 24.

PART IV

SUPPLEMENTARY
MODERN TOPICS

8 The Austrian time–interest equilibrium

Hans Brems[1]

Introduction

Austrian Doctrine

The pioneer of the Austrian time-interest equilibrium was Böhm-Bawerk (1889), who built a flow-input point-output model of circulating capital: over a period of production a uniform flow of input would be applied, and at the end of the period of production, output would materialize. The slow biological growth involved in a business such as a forestry or a winery meant that the concept of time was important. Interest was the price of time, and the demand for time was shown to have a negative interest elasticity: a lower rate of interest would encourage a lengthening of the period of production.

On fixed capital Böhm-Bawerk was silent and so was Wicksell until three years before his death when he (1923) was inspired by Åkerman (1923) to build a point-input flow-output model of fixed capital. At the opening instant a durable producers' good was built. The better it was built the more durable it would be. What took time here was the utilization of buildings or machines. Again the demand for time was shown to have a negative interest elasticity: a lower rate of interest would encourage a lengthening of useful life.

Good history of theory will ask not only if a pioneer's conclusion follows from his own assumptions but also if it would follow from less restrictive assumptions than his. Böhm-Bawerk, Wicksell, and Åkerman assumed absence of inflation and maximized the internal rate of return of a single investment. It would be nice to know if the Austrian time-interest equilibrium would survive the relaxation of those two assumptions: would it hold under inflation and under maximization of the present net worth of an endless succession of investments (avoiding comparing single investments of different lengths)? As it turned out, (Brems, 1988), the Austrian time-interest equilibrium would indeed survive.

The Austrian time-interest equilibrium also assumed technology to be stationary. Would it also survive the relaxation of that assumption? The purpose of this chapter is to see if it would. We shall build the simplest possible optimal-replacement model of the firm assuming first, inflation, second, maximization of the present net worth of an endless succession of investments, and third, embodied technological progress (Johansen, 1959; Solow, 1960 and 1962; and Massell, 1962).

119

Our notation will be the following.

Variables
J   present net worth to a firm of an endless succession of replacements of a single producer's good
P   price of consumers' goods
u   useful life of producers' goods
X   physical output of consumers' goods per annum, per producer's good

Parameters
a_1 labour absorbed in constructing one physical unit of producers' goods
a_2 labour absorbed per annum in operating one physical unit of producers' goods
p   rate of inflation
q   rate of technological progress
r   nominal rate of interest
ρ real rate of interest
w   money wage rate

The model

An endless succession of replacements of a single producer's good
Consider a single producer's good acquired at time *v* and replaced every *u*th year, that is, at times $v + u, v + 2u, \ldots$ forever after. Apply an infinite time horizon and define the present net worth $J(v)$ of such an endless succession as the present worth of all its future revenue *minus* present worth of all its future construction labour *minus* present worth of all its future operating labour. Find the three present worths in turn.

Present worth of all future revenue
Let one producer's good of vintage *t* produce $X(t)$ consumers' goods per annum, and let embodied technological progress manifest itself in a growing $X(t)$, growing over the vintages at the rate *q*:

$$X(t) = \exp [q \, (t-v)] \, X(v) \tag{1}$$

But once installed a producer's good of vintage *v* cannot be altered: steam engines cannot be altered to diesel engines, nor piston planes to jet planes. So once installed, a producer's good of vintage *v* will produce $X(v)$ consumers' goods per annum throughout its useful life. But let that output $X(v)$ be selling at a price $P(t)$ of consumers' goods reflecting latest technology according to (1) available to rivals and entrants, hence be inflating at the rate of inflation p *minus* the rate of technological progress q:

$$P(t) = \exp[(p - q)(t - v)]P(v) \tag{2}$$

Define the real rate of interest as the nominal one *minus* the rate of inflation:

$$\rho \equiv r - p \tag{3}$$

As seen from time v revenue $P(t)X(v)$ at time t is $\exp[-r(t - v)]\, P(t)X(v)$. Insert (2) and (3) and write present worth of all such future revenue throughout the useful life of our single producer's good of vintage v as

$$\int_{v}^{v+u} \exp[-(\rho + q)(t - v)]P(v)X(v)dt = \tag{4}$$
$$\frac{1 - \exp[-(\rho + q)u]}{\rho + q} P(v)X(v)$$

So much for vintage v with its stationary $X(v)$. Let us now go beyond that vintage and consider the ith replacement of it, that is, vintage $v + iu$ of our single producer's good: in (4) replace v by $v + iu$ and write the future worth as seen from $t = v + iu$ of all revenue throughout the useful life of the ith replacement:

$$\frac{1 - \exp[-(\rho + q)u]}{\rho + q} P(v + iu)X(v + iu) \tag{5}$$

Over the vintages $X(t)$ is growing according to (1). So in (1) and (2) replace t by $v + iu$, insert into (5), multiply by $\exp(-iru)$ to see all such revenue from the present time $t = v$ rather than from $t = v + iu$, use (3), and write the present worth of all revenue throughout the useful life of the ith replacement:

$$\frac{1 - \exp[-(\rho + q)u]}{\rho + q} \exp(-i\rho u)P(v)X(v) \tag{6}$$

Finally write (6) successively for $i = 0, 1, 2, \ldots$ Summing over replacements i find the present worth of an endless succession of future revenues

$$\frac{1 - \exp[-(\rho + q)u]}{\rho + q} \frac{P(v)X(v)}{1 - \exp(-\rho u)} \tag{7}$$

Present worth of all future construction labour
Let the length of the construction period of producers' goods be negligible. Let us be truly Ricardian and Wicksellian and assume their construction to require nothing else than labour. Let a_1 be the labour absorbed in constructing one physical unit of producers' goods, and let a_1 be a function of neither economic useful life nor vintage: simply let reliability dictate a physical life always longer

than the economic useful life dictated by obsolescence.

Every *u*th year, say at time *t*, a new vintage will be constructed at a money wage rate inflating at the rate *p*:

$$w(t) = \exp\,[p(t-v)]\,w\,(v) \tag{8}$$

Future construction-labour cost of the *i*th replacement is $a_1w(v + iu)$. In (8) replace *t* by $v + iu$, insert that, multiply by $\exp\,(-iru)$ to see such construction-labour cost from the present time $t = v$ rather than from $t = v + iu$, use (3), and write its present worth

$$a_1\exp\,(-i\rho u)\,w\,(v) \tag{9}$$

Finally write (9) successively for $i = 0, 1, 2, \ldots$ Summing over replacements *i*, find the present worth of an endless succession of future construction labour.

$$\frac{a_1w(v)}{1 - \exp(-\rho u)} \tag{10}$$

Present worth of all future operating labour

Let a_2 be labour absorbed uniformly per annum in operating one physical unit of producers' goods, and let a_2 be a function of neither vintage nor age. As seen from time *v* operating labour cost $a_2w(t)$ at time *t* is $\exp[-r\,(t-v)]\,a_2w(t)$ or, with (3) and (8) inserted, $\exp[-\rho\,(t - v)]\,a_2w(v)$. Present worth of all such future operating labour is then

$$\int_v^\infty \exp[-\rho\,(t - v)]a_2w(v)dt = \frac{a_2w(v)}{\rho} \tag{11}$$

Present net worth of endless succession of replacements

Define present net worth $J(v)$ of our endless succession of replacements as present worth (7) of its future revenue *minus* present worth (10) of its future construction labour *minus* present worth (11) of its future operating labour:

$$J(v) = \frac{1 - \exp[-(\rho + q)u]}{\rho + q}\,\frac{P(v)X(v)}{1 - \exp(-\rho u)} - \frac{a_1w(v)}{1 - \exp(-\rho u)} - \frac{a_2w(v)}{\rho} \tag{12}$$

Optimal useful life: firm equilibrium

'Firm equilibrium' (Burmeister and Dobell, 1970, p. 95) requires the firm to maximize the present net worth of whatever it is about to do. In our case at time *v* the firm is about to install a new physical unit of producers' goods. $J(v)$ of (12) was the present net worth of an endless succession of replacements of such a unit, so the firm must maximize $J(v)$. A first-order condition for such a maximum is

$$\frac{\partial J(v)}{\partial u} = 0 \tag{13}$$

Differentiate (12) with respect to u, treating everything beyond the firm's control as constants, that is, technology a_1, a_2, q, and $X(v)$; the rate of interest ρ; and the wage-price configuration imposed by long-run freedom of entry and exit (see next section). Find the first-order condition for a maximum $J(v)$ to be

$$\frac{\partial J(v)}{\partial u} = \frac{\rho}{\rho + q} \frac{\exp(-\rho u)}{[1 - \exp(-\rho u)]^2} H(v)P(v)X(v) = 0 \tag{14}$$

and satisfied by

$$H(v) \equiv \left[1 + \frac{1 - \exp(-\rho u)}{\rho} q\right] \exp(-qu) - 1 + \frac{a_1 w(v)}{P(v)X(v)} (\rho + q) = 0 \tag{15}$$

Appendix I will show that the second-order condition for a maximum $J(v)$ is satisfied.

Optimal useful life: investment-market equilibrium
Competition in the product market may be nonpure, but in investment markets let competition be pure in the sense that firms expect long-run freedom of entry and exit to impose upon them a wage–price configuration allowing them no more than a zero present net worth. 'Investment-market equilibrium' (Burmeister and Dobell, 1970, p. 95), then, requires not only $J(v)$ to be maximized but also such maximized $J(v)$ to be zero:

$$J(v) = 0 \tag{16}$$

Optimal useful life: full equilibrium
The wage-price configuration still appears in (15) but may be happily eliminated: insert (16) into (12) and express it as

$$\frac{a_1 w(v)}{P(v)X(v)} = \frac{1 - \exp[-(\rho + q)u]}{\{1 + (a_2/a_1)[1 - \exp(-\rho u)]/\rho\}(\rho + q)} \tag{17}$$

Insert (17) into (15), multiply out so -1 and $+1$ may cancel, rearrange and divide away $\exp(-qu) [1 - \exp(-\rho u)]$, and find the full-equilibrium condition collapsing into

$$1 - \exp(qu) + \frac{1 - \exp(-\rho u)}{\rho} q + \frac{a_1}{a_2} (\rho + q) = 0 \tag{18}$$

After the happy elimination of the wage-price configuration, then, optimal useful life u is solely a function of technology a_1, a_2, and q and of the real rate of interest ρ. How sensitive is it to the latter? Considering u a function of ρ, differentiate (18) implicitly with respect to ρ and find the elasticity of useful life u with respect to the real rate of interest ρ:

$$\frac{\partial u}{\partial \rho}\frac{\rho}{u} = \frac{[1 - \exp(-\rho u)(1 + \rho u)]/\rho - (a_1/a_2)(\rho/q)}{[\exp(-\rho u) - \exp(qu)]u} \tag{19}$$

Here for $q > 0$, $\rho > 0$, and $u > 0$ the denominator is always negative. The first term of the numerator is always positive but swamped by the second term for plausible values of a_1/a_2. As a result the elasticity (19) is practically positive. Appendix II discusses the plausible order of magnitude of a_1/a_2.

Let us map the function (18). For a plausible value $a_1/a_2 = 9$ figure 1 maps it in the domains $0.01 < q < 0.05$ and $0.02 < \rho < 0.12$ and shows optimal useful life u to be declining with a rising rate of technological progress q but rising moderately with the real rate of interest ρ – a reversal of Austrian time-interest doctrine.

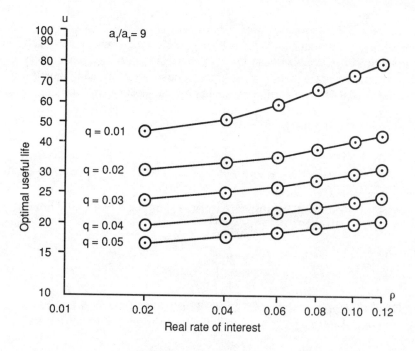

Figure 8.1   Optimal useful life as a function of real rate of interest

Conclusion

Breaking out of the stationary technology of the Austrians, we have built an optimal-replacement model showing a positive but moderate interest elasticity of useful life.

We have kept our model very simple and may restate it intuitively as follows. Vintages older than v had a productivity less than $X(v)$ and could no longer be altered. For example, if technological progress were, say, 2 per cent per annum and useful life, say, 32 years, then the productivity of vintage $v - 32$, about to be replaced, would be only slightly over half the productivity of vintage v replacing it. Replacing equipment too rarely, then, would waste labour on operating obsolescent equipment. Replacing too frequently, on the other hand, would waste capital on throw-away extravagance. A balance must be found, and a lower rate of interest would tilt the balance in favour of more frequent replacement, that is, shorter useful life, thus reversing Austrian time-interest doctrine.

We have also kept our model very pure. From reswitching we have isolated it by assuming uniformity of output and operating-labour input throughout useful life. From capital deepening we have isolated it by assuming fixed labour-input coefficients, as did Solow, Tobin, von Weizsäcker, and Yaari (1966, pp. 79–80).

Appendix I. Second-order condition for a maximum $J(v)$

To prove that the second-order condition for a maximum $J(v)$ is satisfied, differentiate (14) with respect to u:

$$\frac{\partial^2 J(v)}{\partial u^2} = \frac{\rho}{\rho + q}\, P(v)X(v)\, \frac{\exp(-\rho u)}{[1 - \exp(-\rho u)]^2}\, \frac{\partial H}{\partial u}$$

$$+ \frac{\rho}{\rho + q}\, P(v)X(v)H\partial \left\{\frac{\exp(-\rho u)}{[1 - \exp(-\rho u)]^2}\right\} / \partial u$$

But according to (15) $H = 0$, so

$$\frac{\partial^2 J(v)}{\partial u^2} = -\frac{\exp[-(\rho + q)u]}{1 - \exp(-\rho u)}\, qP(v)X(v)$$

which is always negative.

Appendix II. Plausible order of magnitude of a_1/a_2

Multiply numerator and denominator of a_1/a_2 by $w(v)/[P(v)X(v)]$:

$$\frac{a_1}{a_2} \equiv \frac{a_1 w(v)}{P(v)X(v)} \bigg/ \frac{a_2 w(v)}{P(v)X(v)}$$

and find it to be incremental capital coefficient divided by incremental labour's share in the consumers' goods industry. Is there a real-life counterpart to it?

Our producers' goods industry had a labour's share of one. Let the consumers' goods industry have an average labour's share of, say, 7/10. Let the gross investment share of overall output be, say, 1/6 (Kuznets, 1966, p. 237). That would make labour's overall share a plausible 3/4 (Kuznets, 1966, p. 80).

But we need incremental labour's share in the consumers' goods industry, not the average share 7/10. An incremental labour's share on the latest, most productive, vintage is obviously lower than the average share on all vintages present in the physical capital stock. At realistic values of growth rates, useful lives, and rates of technological progress incremental share may be, say, 7/9 of average share, thus equalling $(7/9)(7/10) = 49/90$. Finally let the incremental capital coefficient in the consumers' goods industry be, say, 4.9 (Kuznets, 1966, p. 254). Then $a_1/a_2 = 4.9/(49/90) = 9$.

Note

1.   To solve our transcendental equation (18) for small values of p and q a modification of the Newton–Raphson method was desirable. For such modification and for computing the solution the author is indebted to Dr. Daniel P. Connors of IBM and James Perkins of the Coordinated Science Laboratory of the University of Illinois. For helpful comments the author is indebted to members of workshops at the Stockholm Industrial Institute for Economic and Social Research, at the University of Gothenburg, at Denmark's Institute of Technology, and at the Catholic University of Leuven.

References

Åkerman, G. (1923), *Realkapital und Kapitalzins,* Stockholm: Centraltryckeriet.
Böhm-Bawerk, E. von (1889), *Positive Theorie des Kapitales,* Innsbruck: Wagner'sche Universitäts-Buchhandlung, translated by William Smart (1891), as *Positive Theory of Capital,* London and New York: Macmillan.
Brems, H. (1988), 'Time and interest: Böhm-Bawerk and Åkerman–Wicksell,' *History of Political Economy,* **20**, pp. 565–81.
Burmeister, E., and Dobell, A. R. (1970), *Mathematical Theories of Economic Growth,* New York: Macmillan.
Johansen, L. (1959), 'Substitution versus fixed production coefficients in the theory of economic growth: A synthesis', *Econometrica,* **27**, pp. 157–76.
Kuznets, S. (1966), *Modern Economic Growth,* New Haven: Yale University Press.
Massell, B. F. (1962), 'Investment, innovation, and growth', *Econometrica,* **30**, pp. 239–52.
Solow, R. M. (1959), 'Investment and technical progress', in Arrow, K. J., *et al.* (eds), *Mathematical Methods in the Social Sciences,* Stanford, California: Stanford University Press.
Solow, R. M. (1962), 'Technical progress, capital formation and economic growth', *American Economic Review,* **52**, pp. 76–86.
Solow, R. M., Tobin, J. von Weizsäcker, C. C. and Yaari, M. (1966), 'Neoclassical growth with fixed factor proportions', *Review of Economic Studies,* **33**, pp. 79–115.
Wicksell, K. (1923), 'Realkapital och kapitalränta', *Ekonomisk Tidskrift,* **25**, pp. 145–80, translated by Solomon Adler as Appendix 2, 'Real capital and interest', in Wicksell, K. *Lectures on Political Economy,* I, London: Routledge & Kegan Paul. (Reprinted 1967.)

9 Wicksell's Wicksell effect, the price Wicksell effect, and the real Wicksell effect

Bo Sandelin

Introduction

In the so-called Cambridge controversy on capital, the *price Wicksell effect* and the *real Wicksell effect* were two important concepts. It is sometimes suggested that the effect in Wicksell's own writings is equivalent to a *price* Wicksell effect, and a strong form of this proposition is found in Ferguson and Hooks (1971; cf. Ferguson, 1972) who say that 'the real Wicksell effect does not appear in Wicksell in any guise'.

In this chapter, we will clarify how the *price* Wicksell effect and the *real* Wicksell effect apply to Wicksell's own analysis in the wine example in *Lectures on Political Economy,* vol.1. We will establish that there is both a *price* Wicksell effect and a *real* Wicksell effect in Wicksell's 'last portion of capital'. The *price* Wicksell effect coincides with what Uhr (1951) originally called merely the Wicksell effect.

Added to the *real* Wicksell effect, the *price* Wicksell effect makes the marginal product of capital in Wicksell's analysis less than the rate of return. (Sometimes this difference between the marginal product of capital and the rate of return has been called the Wicksell effect. In the following we ignore this usage and stick to the customary terminology.)

Wicksell's analysis

First, let us summarize Wicksell's own analysis in *Lectures*. The amount of labour is given. We do not violate any of Wicksell's critical assumptions if we assume that the equations are specified on a per capita basis.

A point input–point output technique is applied in a one-good economy; 'a concrete example of this kind is to be found in the laying down of wine for consumption... or alternatively in the planting of trees on barren land' (p. 172). Thus

$$q = f(t); \; f'(t) > 0 \tag{1}$$

where q is output per head per period and t is the time which has elapsed since input. If the cost of input, that is, the wage rate, is denoted by w, the rate of return equals r in

$$q = we^{rt} \tag{2}$$

Wicksell assumes maximization of the rate of return, r, which yields the following first-order condition

$$q'/q = r \tag{3}$$

Capital goods are goods in process like the cultivation of wine or growing trees. Their value per head, k, equals the capitalized cost of input; capitalization is performed by means of the prevailing rate of return. Thus, in a stationary state with continuous input and output,

$$k = w \int_0^t e^{rx} dx = \frac{we^{rt} - w}{r} \tag{4}$$

Equations (1)–(4) constitute the model. Differentiation of the system of equations yields, after a certain amount of substitution,

$$\frac{dq}{dk} = r + (k - wt) \frac{dr}{dk} \tag{5}$$

dq, dk, and dr can be interpreted as differences in the values of the variables between two adjacent stationary states. As (4) holds and the rate of return in (4) may be assumed to be positive, the parenthesis in (5) is positive. It can be shown that $dr/dk < 0$. Therefore,

$$\frac{dq}{dk} < r \tag{6}$$

The marginal product of capital is less than the rate of return, when the marginal product is defined by comparing two adjacent stationary states with respect to output and the value of capital. The phenomenon which causes this inequality was termed the *Wicksell effect* by Uhr (1951).

The price Wicksell effect and the real Wicksell effect
Later on, during the 'Cambridge controversy', the concepts of a *price* Wicksell effect and a *real* Wicksell effect were introduced. Let us reproduce the definition of these concepts in Harcourt's (1972) now classic book: 'The *price* Wicksell effect relates to changes in the value of capital as w and r change their values but techniques do not change, i.e. it is associated with the w–r relationship that corresponds to *one* technique. *Real* Wicksell effects relate to changes in the value of capital associated with changes in techniques as w and r take on dif-

ferent values, i.e. they are differences in the values of capital at (or, rather, very near) switch points on the envelope of the w–r relationships' (p. 40).

The w–r curve or factor price curve, for a certain technique shows the highest possible wage rate for a given rate of return when that technique is applied, or, the highest possible rate of return for a given wage rate. In a point input – point output model, consisting of equations (1), (2), and (4), the slope of the w–r curve is negative, but less negative the lower is w. Differentiating (2) we get

$$dq = \exp(rt)dw + wt\exp(rt) \, dr + wr\exp(rt) \, dt \tag{7}$$

However, for a given technique dq and dt equal zero. Taking this into account, and rearranging terms in (7), we get

$$\frac{dw}{dr} = -wt \tag{7a}$$

which confirms the statement above about the slope of the w–r curve.

Figure 9.1(b) demonstrates the relationship between output per head, q, and the time span between input and output, t. Figure 9.1(a) depicts the w–r curve for the technique with time span t_1. It is related to Figure 9.1(b) in the following way.

On the ordinate axis in Figure 9.1(b), different wage rates are marked. For each of these wage rates, there is a rate of return such that a $w\exp(rt)$ curve cuts the q curve above t_1, thus indicating that equation (2) is satisfied. The combinations of such ws and rs constitute the curve in Figure 9.1(a) which, consequently, shows the highest possible r for given w, when the technique with time span t_1 between input and output is applied. For wage rate w_1^3 no interest is obtained, and $w_1^3 = q_1$

Combining (2) and (4), we get

$$k = \frac{q - w}{r} \tag{8}$$

That means that in Figure 9.1(a) the value of capital per head corresponds to the absolute slope of a straight line from the actual point on the w–r curve to the point on the ordinate axis where the w–r curve reaches the axis. (Cf. Harcourt, p. 41). Thus, for (r_1^1, w_1^1) the value of capital per head equals

$$\frac{q_1^1 - w_1^1}{r_1^1}$$

When the w–r curve is convex to the origin, as in Figure 9.1(a), the absolute slope of a straight line from the curve to the ordinate axis where the axis is reached by the curve increases when r decreases. Thus, k increases when r decreases. This implies a positive *price* Wicksell effect.

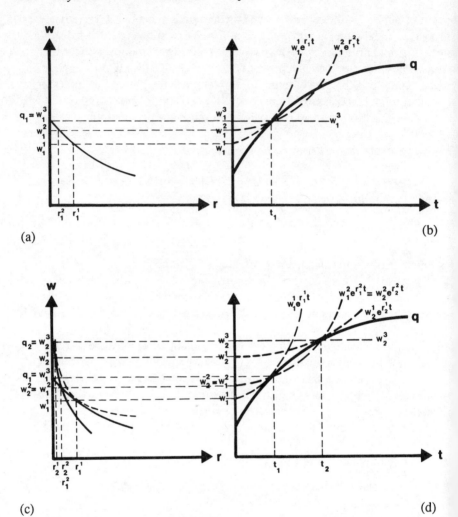

Figure 9.1

The *w–r* curve in Figure 9.1(a) presupposes *one* technique, characterized by time span t_1 from input to output, and by output per head equal to q_1. We can, of course, draw other *w–r* curves for other techniques.

In Figure 9.1(d) we have added a case with a new technique, characterized by time span t_2 and output q_2 per head. The corresponding *w–r* curve in Figure 9.1(c) is steeper than the *w–r* curve for t_1. It reaches the ordinate axis at a higher level $q_2 = w_2^3$. It crosses the *w–r* curve for t_1 at wage rate $w_2^2 = w_1^2$ and rate of return $r_2^2 = r_1^2$. The *w*exp(rt) curve for these values of *w* and *r* in Figure 9.1(d) crosses the output curve both at time span t_1 and t_2.

The real Wicksell effect and the price Wicksell effect in Wicksell's complete model

It is possible to construct many *w–r* curves, one for each *t*. The envelope of all such curves is indicated by the dotted curve in Figure 9.1(c). Our two fully drawn *w–r* curves coincide with the envelope at (r_1^T, w_1^1) and (r_2^1, w_2^1), respectively. The *w*exp(rt) curves in Figure 9.1(b) and 9.1(d), corresponding to these two points, are tangents to the output curve at time span t_1 and t_2, respectively. At such points of tangence equation (3) in Wicksell's model is also satisfied; no other adjacent technique yields a higher *r* at the actual *w*. This implies that the envelope curve in Figure 9.1(c) shows the highest possible *r* for each *w* (or the highest possible *w* for each *r*) when the technique is *not* constant but optimally chosen.

In Wicksell's complete model, a solution corresponds to a point of tangence between a *w*exp(rt) curve and the output curve in Figures 9.1(b) and 9.1(d), and to a point on the envelope curve in Figure 9.1(c). After some vacillation, Wicksell regards the value of capital as an exogenous variable. Thus, in the model consisting of the four equations (1)–(4), *q*, *w*, *r*, and *t* are endogenous variables and *k* is exogenous.

Wicksell considers the consequences of going from one stationary state to an adjacent one with more capital. In his arithmetic example, capital is increased from 314 to 422 million shillings which gives rise to an increased annual yield of 10 million shillings; in his algebraic formulation the corresponding result is expressed in equation (5).

This is also illustrated in Figure 9.1. We start with an original stationary state characterized by t_1, w_1^1, r_1^1, q_1, and capital per head

$$k_1 = \frac{q_1 - w_1^1}{r_1^1}$$

We compare this stationary state with an adjacent one (although, for the sake of diagrammatic clarity we interpret adjacency generously), characterized by $t_2, w_2^1, r_2^1, q_2,$

and

$$k_2 = \frac{q_2 - w_2^1}{r_2^1}$$

The difference between k_2 and k_1 (that is, between the slopes of a straight line from the actual point on the w–r curve in question to the intercept of that curve on the ordinate axis) is in part due to the fact that we compare points on two different w–r curves. Hence, there is at least a *real* Wicksell effect in Wicksell's 'last portion of capital', or 'increase in *social* capital', although the term 'real effect' is absent in Wicksell's analysis.

Is there a *price* Wicksell effect, too? Strictly speaking, in the complete version of Wicksell's model, it is impossible that 'w and r change their values but techniques do not change'. A model consisting of equations (1), (2), and (4) would permit different combinations of w and r for each technique, but as soon as equation (3) is added only *one* combination of w and r is possible for each technique, namely that which makes a $wexp^{rt}$ curve be a tangent to the q curve at the point corresponding to the technique in question.

However, if we interpret 'techniques do not change' less literally, as I think we should, or, if, as is often done (for example, in Burmeister, 1980, p. 123), we express a *price* Wicksell effect as $z \cdot dp$ in

$$dk = z \cdot dp + p \cdot dz \tag{9}$$

(where z is the physical amount of capital and p is the value of capital per physical unit), there is obviously both a *price* Wicksell effect and a *real* Wicksell effect inherent in Wicksell's 'last portion of capital'. We can provide further evidence for this proposition:

The *price* and the *real* Wicksell effects in Wicksell's model can be illustrated not only in Figures 9.1(a) and 9.1(c), but also in Figures 9.1(b) and 9.1(d). However, to avoid too cluttered a figure, we draw a new one, Figure 9.2. In accordance with equation (4), the value of capital equals the area under the $wexp^{rt}$ curve from the current t-value to $t = 0$. Two adjacent stationary states differ in the value of capital, because both the physical amount and the value of each unit differ. The former difference is related to the *real* Wicksell effect, the latter to the *price* Wicksell effect. Disregarding second-order magnitudes (which, it must be confessed, are considerable when the two states are so far from each other as in Figure 9.2), the total difference in the value of capital can be divided into a *real* Wicksell effect and a *price* Wicksell effect as in Figure 9.2. The *price* Wicksell effect area corresponds to $z \cdot dp$ in (9) and to what Uhr (1951) termed just the Wicksell effect; it illustrates Swan's (1956) proposition that the Wicksell effect – that is, the *price* Wicksell effect – 'is nothing but an inventory revaluation'. The core of this phenomenon can also be illustrated in a much simpler model than Wicksell's wine model(Sandelin, 1989).

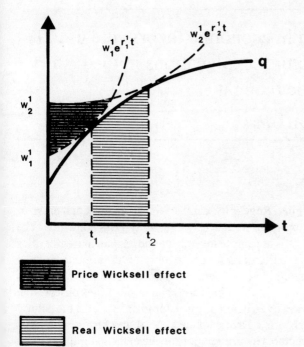

Price Wicksell effect

Real Wicksell effect

Figure 9.2

Conclusions

In equation (5), *dk* is the sum of a *price* Wicksell effect and a *real* Wicksell effect. Therefore, it is questionable to ascribe only a *price* Wicksell effect to Wicksell's own analysis. Especially, an assertion that 'the real Wicksell effect does not appear in Wicksell in any guise' is erroneous.

References

Burmeister, E. (1980), *Capital Theory and Dynamics*, New York: Cambridge University Press.

Ferguson, C.E. (1972), 'The Current State of Capital Theory: A Tale of two Paradigms', *Southern Economic Journal*, 39.

Ferguson, C.E., and Hooks, D.L. (1971), 'The Wicksell Effects in Wicksell and in Modern Capital Theory', *History of Political Economy*, 3.

Harcourt, G.C. (1972), *Some Cambridge Controversies in the Theory of Capital*, Cambridge: Cambridge University Press.

Sandelin, B. (1989), 'Knight's Crusonia Plant – A Short Cut to the Wicksell Effect', *History of Political Economy*, 21.

Swan, T.W. (1956), 'Economic Growth and Capital Accumulation', *Economic Record*, 32.

Uhr, C.G. (1951), 'Knut Wicksell – A Centennial Evaluation', *American Economic Review*, 41.

Wicksell, K. (1977), *Lectures on Political Economy*, vol. 1, translation of third Swedish edition (1928), New York: A.M. Kelley.

10 Naturalism in economic theory: the use of 'state of nature' explanations in the history of economic thought

Charles M. A. Clark[1]

All theory presupposes order. Regularities and uniformities must first exist, or at least be perceived to exist, before theoretical activity can commence. The object of theoretical activity is not only to investigate and explain the regularities but also to inquire into the source of these regularities. It is the argument of this chapter that, under the natural law outlook, mainstream economic theory has looked to nature as the source of the regularities and uniformities observed in economic phenomena. Moreover, based on the naturalism aspect of the natural law outlook, economic theorists have excluded social and historical factors from their theoretical structures in an attempt to arrive at the natural forces. In so much as economic theory has abstracted from these non-natural factors, it has, like many of the Enlightenment social theorists, relied heavily on 'state of nature' explanations. Viewed in this light, the specific form of abstraction used in economic theory emerges as an attempt to explain social phenomena as if it were, like natural phenomena, the result of natural forces.

The argument will be organized as follows. The chapter begins with a brief sketch of the natural law outlook, paying particular attention to the naturalism aspect of natural law theories. In section II, Hobbes and the function of 'state of nature' explanations will be examined. Section III reviews the role of 'state of nature' explanations in Adam Smith, and shows how Smith's analysis went beyond naturalism. In section IV the naturalism implicit in the marginal utility revolution will be discussed, illustrating both the continuity and discontinuity with the naturalism of the classical economists. Finally, we will look at modern general equilibrium theory and the use of axiomatic theorizing as a type of 'state or nature' explanation *sans* nature.

I

The influence of 'laws of nature' and the natural law philosophers on classical political economy has been much studied.[2] Our present concern is not with the particular natural law theories, but with the natural law outlook. The main object of classical economic theory was to discover the natural laws as they pertained to economic phenomena. This is no less true for the economists of the marginal utility revolution (Clark, 1989b). Veblen's (1919, p. 61) insightful comments on the classicals is equally applicable to the neoclassicals:

> [F]or the classical economists, ... [the] ... ground of cause and effect is not definitive.... The ultimate term in their systematization of knowledge is a 'natural law'. This natural law is felt to exercise some sort of a coercive surveillance over the sequence of events, and to give a spiritual stability and consistence to the causal relation at any given juncture. To meet the high classical requirement, a sequence – and a development process especially – must be apprehended in terms of a consistent propensity tending to some spiritually legitimate end. When facts and events have been reduced to these terms of fundamental truth and have been made to square with the requirements of definitive normality, the investigator rests his case. Any causal sequence which is apprehended to traverse the imputed propensity in events is a 'disturbing factor'.

Essential to the natural law outlook are three distinct postulates: the existence of a social physics; naturalism (the origin in nature of these laws); and the derivation of a natural moral theory from the discovery of the natural laws.

Social physics
Natural law theories have as their foundation the idea or a natural order – that material phenomena display an underlying order which is the result of universal natural laws. In the natural sciences this idea has led to the search for regularities in the physical universe and has been very successful. Natural law theories hold that the social universe also is ordered by universal natural laws, hence social theorists ought to search for a social physics.

Naturalism
As pointed out by Schumpeter (1954, p. 110), 'there is [an] association of natural law with primitive conditions'; that is, natural law theories regard nature as a final cause. Naturalism is the belief that nature is the source of regularities and uniformities, and hence laws, and that a scientific explanation must explain phenomena at the level of its natural cause. Furthermore, nature is to be found by abstracting from society. Naturalism manifests itself in two ways: analysis of innate human nature and the reliance on 'state of nature' explanations to illuminate the origins and functions of social phenomena.

Natural moral theory
The existence of theories of natural social laws which regulate human activity developed hand in hand with the search for moral laws based on nature.[3] In fact the former was developed to demonstrate the latter. Natural laws of social behaviour are also moral laws and thus any interference by human institutions would not only be counter-productive but unnatural.[4]

The creation of economics as a scientific pursuit, under the preconceptions of the time as to what 'scientific' meant, led to the search for nature as a final cause for all theories.[5] From its earliest formulations economics has sought to be 'scientific' which, for each era, meant to emulate the methods of what was then considered science. A brief look at Adam Smith will demonstrate this point. Smith defined philosophy as the 'science of the connecting principles of nature' (Smith, 1979, p. 45), and in analysing competing scientific methods claimed that the Newtonian method was the superior one (Smith, 1983, pp. 145–6). Thus like Newton, Smith searched for the laws of nature by investigating nature, as well as basing his system on Newton's model. Under the natural law outlook, particularly in its Enlightenment manifestation, social phenomena were deemed to be the result of universal laws which were implanted in human nature.[6] Human nature was the final cause for the social sciences just as nature had been the final cause for the physical sciences.

II

In order to arrive at social theories based on human nature one must ascertain precisely what constitutes human nature. Since we are searching for natural forces we must consider only those aspects of human behaviour which are 'natural' and exclude all those which are not natural – that is, social factors. This method of analysis is the essence of 'state of nature' explanations, and it has its origins in Thomas Hobbes.

In the *Leviathan*, Hobbes not only posed the question which was to dominate social inquiry for the Enlightenment (whence social order?), but more importantly, he provided the framework with which social inquiry was to take place. Hobbes constructed his theory of social order by first investigating those aspects of man's behaviour which are natural and not the result of social influences. To do this, Hobbes constructed a model of man as he is in a state of nature – independent of social influences. Although Hobbes's theory of social order was almost universally rejected by the Enlightenment, most social theorists accepted the form of his argument. Theories of social order (or more generally social theory) should start with the nature of the individual (human nature). Furthermore, human nature was to be considered universal and constant, independent of social influences – such as customs, history and institutions. Commenting on Hobbes's method, Milton L. Myers (1983, p. 30) has noted:

> He begins his study of man by stripping away the disguising and obscuring paraphernalia of social life in order to see man in his natural and essential state. Hobbes removes man from institutions and customs, hoping to see him as he really is. His method might, in a sense, be likened to the mathematical because he is subtracting elements from what makes up the totality of man's condition and nature, the remainder being the denominator common to all individuals.

Myers's use of the mathematical analogy is particularly applicable to Hobbes and his lasting influence on social thought. Hobbes felt that his method of reasoning was merely mathematics. In the *Leviathan*, Hobbes wrote that 'when a man reasoneth, hee does nothing else but conceive a summe totall, from addition of parcels; or conceive a remainder, from subtraction of one summe from another' (Hobbes, 1964, p. 22). Even in the mid-seventeenth century social theorists equated scientific thought with mathematics.

The philosophers who attacked Hobbes's contention of the need for a strong central government did so by arguing that either man's nature was not anti-social, the point made by Richard Cumberland who argues that trade and self-interest led to a social equilibrium of sorts, or, by asserting, as did John Locke, that man in a state of nature has natural rights, and thus forms government to protect these rights. Hobbes thus fosters the naturalistic view of the social universe (although this was present in many Greek philosophers, especially the Stoics). Together with the Copernican Revolution in the natural sciences, they brought forth a new vision of the universe. The natural law outlook of the Middle Ages, in which divine revelation was the final standard of what constituted a natural law, was replaced with a 'scientific' natural law outlook. God was still the final cause, yet the reliance on revelation was replaced by reason (Descartes) or by observation (Newton). Whether one was a Cartesian or a Newtonian, the world was viewed as ordered by a grand design, and the role of science was to figure out the laws that regulated it. Under the principle of design, both the social and the natural universe were regulated by natural laws. Thus the same method of analysis is applicable to both the natural and social sciences.

III

Adam Smith undoubtedly held the natural law outlook but it is equally true that his system goes well beyond and, in fact, makes an implicit break with the natural law outlook (Clark, 1990). Yet in Smith we still find a reliance on naturalism. What is perplexing is that Smith realizes the limitations of Hobbes's approach, stating that there is 'no purpose to treat the laws which take place in a state of nature,... as there is no such state existing' (Smith, 1978, p. 398). Yet Smith relies heavily on 'state of nature' explanations as a starting point for many of his key theories. The contradiction arises because of his concern for both efficient and final causes.[7] Smith's naturalism comes from his search for final causes, yet Newtonian and Natural Theological influences led him to search for final causes through investigating efficient causes. According to Newton and Natural Theology the only way one can discover the laws of nature is by investigating their manifestations in the real world. Thus it is essential to Smith that his analysis of final causes to some extent be empirically grounded. Smith's naturalism is apparent in many aspects of his work. All explanations are based on human nature or on social institutions which are the result of the innate human propensities. The composition of human nature, for Smith and the Scottish Enlightenment, was universal, naturally determined and unchanging.[8]

Smith's economic theory is based on the propensities to truck, barter and exchange and to better one's condition. His ethics are based on 'some principle in ... [human nature], which interests him in the fortune of others, and render their happiness necessary to him' (Smith, 1976a, p. 9); whence comes the sympathy principle. Smith's philosophical essays explain scientific inquiry by means of natural propensities, relating to both the motivation to search for explanations, and to the criteria by which explanations are deemed satisfactory. Here Smith gives a theory of scientific inquiry, based on human nature:[9] the sentiments of Wonder, Surprise and Admiration. It is because these sentiments are disturbed and aroused that scientific inquiry is undertaken; the superior theory is one which best settles these sentiments.

> Philosophy, by representing the invisible chains which bind together all these disjointed objects, endeavours to introduce order into this chaos of jarring and discordant appearances, to allay this tumult of the imagination, and to restore it, when it surveys the great revolutions of the universe, to that tone of tranquillity and composure, which is both most agreeable in itself, and most suitable to its nature (Smith, 1979, pp. 45–6).

Even the formation of languages is derived from what James Becker has termed the propensity to classify.

> Mankind are naturally disposed to give to one object the name of any other, which nearly resembles it, and thus to denominate a multitude, by what originally was intended to express an individual (Smith, 1983, p. 204).[10]

We saw in the beginning of this chapter that an important aspect of naturalism is the use of 'state of nature' explanations. The most prominent use of 'state of nature' explanations by Smith is in his economics, where we frequently find that his analysis of a fundamental topic begins with a discussion of the early and rude state of society. Smith begins his exposition of the natural laws which regulate exchange with a 'state of nature' explanation of exchange in pre-society.

> In that early and rude state of society which proceeds both the accumulation of stock and the appropriation of land, the proportion between the quantities of labour necessary for acquiring different objects seems to be the only circumstance which can afford any rule for exchanging them one for another. If among a nation of hunters, for example, it usually costs twice the labour to kill a beaver which it does to kill a deer, one beaver should naturally exchange for or be worth two deer. It is natural that what is usually the produce of two days or hours labour, should be worth

double of what is usually the produce of one days or one hour's labour (Smith, 1976b, p. 65).

Similarly, his 'Considerations Concerning the First Formation of Languages' starts with such a situation:

Two savages, who had never been taught to speak, but had been bred up remote from the societies of man, would naturally begin to form that language by which they would endeavor to make their mutual wants intelligible to each other (Smith, 1983, p. 203; see also p. 9).

Such 'state of nature' explanations were the starting point for Smith's conjectural history. On conjectural history Dugald Stewart wrote:

In this want of direct evidence, we are under a necessity of supplying the place of fact by conjecture; and when we are unable to ascertain how men have actually conducted themselves upon particular occasions, of considering in what manner they are likely to have proceeded, from the principles of their nature, and the history of mankind, as well as in examining the phenomena of the material world when we cannot trace the process by which an event *has been* produced, it is often of importance to be able to show how it *may have been* produced by natural causes ... from known principles of human nature (Stewart in Smith, 1979, p. 293, emphases in original).

Conjectural history arises out of the naturalism aspect of the natural law outlook.[11]

Naturalism is apparent in Smith's theories in that all action is based on nature. When Smith is describing final causes humans react mechanically to the stimulus of differential gain according to their natural drives and propensities. Yet, in his analysis of efficient causes, Smith develops an analysis of human behaviour which is the result of social forces. Here we find in Smith an implicit break with the natural law outlook: naturalism for society is the result of an evolutionary process and human behaviour the result of the socialization process. Yet Smith does not perceive his analysis of efficient causes – social institutions and history – as a break with the search for natural laws. The study of society was how one discovered the final causes (the natural laws).

IV

The marginal utility revolution dramatically changed many aspects of economic theory. Following Donald Winch (1972), one could argue that the most important modification made by the marginalists was to the boundaries of economic science. The marginalists were greater prisoners to the natural law outlook than the classical economists in that they were of the opinion that pure theory must exclude historical and social factors. They were thus more consistent in their belief in the natural law outlook, and for our present concern, the naturalism aspect of the natural law outlook.[12]

Leon Walras is a typical example of this trend. For Walras, pure economics is not only regulated by natural laws, its primary elements are also based on nature.[13] This is seen most clearly in Walras's treatment of value, which for him is caused and determined by natural forces.

> Maximum effective utility on the one hand; uniformity of price, on the other hand; ... constitute the double condition by which the universe of economic interests is automatically governed; just as the universe of astronomical movements is automatically governed by ... gravitation ... In one case as in the other, the whole science is contained in a formula ... which serves to explain a countless multitude of particular phenomena. Furthermore ... the mechanism of free competition is a self-driven and self-regulating mechanism (Walras, 1954, p. 305).

And he further states:

> [A]ny value in exchange, once established, partakes of the character of a natural phenomenon, natural in its origins, natural in its manifestations, and natural in essence ... (for things to) have any value at all, it is because they are scarce, that is useful and limited in quantity – both conditions being natural (ibid, p. 69).

All three of the original marginalists went to great lengths to place nature as the final cause of the economic forces which bring about the natural laws.[14] They were thus consistent with the naturalism inherent in natural law theories. Yet the naturalism of the marginalists is most evident in the role of exchange in their systems. The marginalists established the act of exchange as the core activity with which economic theory was to concern itself. It was in the act of exchange that the natural laws of the economy were to be discovered, and thus all their theories were merely theories of exchange and extensions of their theory of exchange.

What seems to have been missed by historians of economic thought is that the marginalists' concentration on exchange is merely a new manifestation of the 'state of nature' explanation tool in social theory. All the marginalists felt that exchange must be analysed independent of society.[15] What is being observed is the natural behaviour of two individuals acting independent of society. This is best demonstrated in the Edgeworth Box, in which we find two individuals possessing only their autonomous and original preferences and their initial endowments (where these endowments come from must be excluded from the analysis for this will necessarily bring in society) and, based on their natural desire to maximize their utility, trading with each other until they reach the contract curve. The object of the Edgeworth Box analysis is to model natural behaviour, excluding society.

Another example of the use of 'state of nature' explanations in marginal utility economics is the use of Robinson Crusoe stories to explain economic activity. Robinson Crusoe is the neo-classical counterpart to the seventeenth-century noble savage, alone in the state of nature, independent of society, living in pre-society. Such explanations are designed to demonstrate the natural laws of human nature. Here we see a second example of the naturalism in marginalists' theories.

Similar to Smith, the marginalists constructed their theories based on natural factors. Yet there is an essential difference between Smith and the marginalists. Smith's method of discovering the natural laws was based on an investigation of society – of efficient causes. The marginalists, however, rely exclusively on an *a priori* knowledge of human nature. They are clear in stating the uselessness of the study of society in an understanding of human nature, yet they offer no empirical analysis to justify their conception of human nature. Jevons merely adopts Bentham's Utilitarianism, while Menger relies on introspection for his knowledge of human nature. In Walras's theory, humans are so lifeless that they are almost assumed away, yet he does claim that diminishing marginal utility is a natural force. Thus, unlike Smith, they make no effort to establish an empirical basis of their conception of human nature. Their natural law pre-conceptions provide them with a model of man which they accept uncritically (Clark, 1989b). Yet they are confident in the validity of their views on nature and human nature.

Jevons's sunspot theory of the business cycle is a good example of the tendency of the marginalists to look for natural forces regulating economic phenomena. As Philip Mirowski has noted (1989, p. 49) this attempt to explain economic phenomena as determined by natural forces has implicit the idea of a 'natural economy', an economy exhibiting the structure and institutions which natural forces would create and free of those that social forces would impose. This of course is the natural order and such an analysis must necessarily be of the 'state of nature' variety.

V

Modern neoclassical economic theory has its origins, in terms of its formal structure, in the analysis of exchange put forth by Jevons, Menger and Walras, and generalized by Walras and Pareto into general equilibrium theory. An analysis of the natural law foundations of equilibrium theory is beyond the scope of this chapter.[16] We must look briefly, however, at the method of general equilibrium. Economics as an exact science is intimately connected with the concept of equilibrium.[17] Neo-classical economic theory gives primary attention to equilibrium. All theoretical investigations start with the quest to demonstrate the existence, stability and optimality of equilibrium. This accomplished, all phenomena are understood in relation to equilibrium positions.

Processes are either equilibrating or disequilibrating. The overriding assumption, on which this whole method is based, is the theoretical importance of equilibrium positions.

The progressive development of the general equilibrium theory and method has centred on the three problems of the existence, stability and optimality of equilibrium. The success with which modern general equilibrium theorists have demonstrated these characteristics of equilibrium has mainly been the result of the application of mathematics and the axiomatic method. The axiomatic method of analysis consists of stating explicitly well-defined axioms from which a logically consistent set of theorems and hypotheses are derived. Both the theorems and the axioms are independent of real world counterparts and interpretation. In fact this independence from reality is considered by proponents to be a strength of the axiomatic method. Debreu defends the use of the axiomatic method in the introduction to his *Theory of Value* (1959, p. x):

> Allegiance to rigor dictates the axiomatic form of the analysis where the theory, in the strict sense, is logically entirely disconnected from its interpretation.... Such a dichotomy reveals all the assumptions and the logical structure of the analysis. It also makes possible immediate extensions of that analysis without modification of the theory by simple reinterpretations of the concepts.

The adoption of the axiomatic method is a further narrowing of the boundaries of economics.[18] For our present purpose we will limit our attention to the question of naturalism. With the development of an axiomatic theory of value, Debreu and his followers have broken with the idea of grounding economic theory on nature and natural forces. The axioms with which they build their theories, as well as their theories themselves, are completely divorced from any real world counterpart or interpretation. As Ingrao and Israel (1985, pp. 91–2) have noted:

> [the axiomatic method,] following the canons of formalism ... radically and uncompromisingly empties the theory of any empirical reference ... Debreu's interpretation of general economic equilibrium theory makes it a self-sufficient formal structure which loses even the feature of being a 'model' at all. The concepts of the theory are no longer understood as the outcome of a process of abstracting from real phenomena, nor as the formalism of 'ideas and knowledge relating to a phenomenon'. Neither do they require empirical verification to prove the validity. ... The dichotomy between mathematical structure and the interpretative content of that structure strips general economic equilibrium theory once and for all of its ambition to provide an interpretative scheme to analyze the functioning of an economy of competitive markets.

General equilibrium theory, in its axiomatic form, is thus a peculiar type of 'state of nature' explanation in that it has abstracted society out of consideration and it explains economic order as the result of the assumed behaviour patterns of autonomous individual economic actors. Yet its axioms are not claimed to be natural forces.[19] The axioms are derived from neither society nor nature. They instead are the axioms which provide for the desired end result of the theory, the determination of the existence, stability and optimality of economic equilibrium in a competitive economy.

VI

Schumpeter argued that the determination of the existence, stability and optimality of equilibrium was of paramount importance, regardless of the level of abstraction. The solution of these three problems is the two hundred year old search for the Invisible Hand – 'can a decentralized economy relying only on price signals for market information be orderly?' (Hahn, 1981, p. 126). The question of economic order is at the same time the question of social order. Smith tried to demonstrate the order in a market economy by analysing both the efficient and final causes which determined the order. Thus Smith uses nature as a final cause and society as the efficient cause. In Smith naturalism and 'state of nature' explanations are used but they do not compose the whole foundation of his system. For the marginalists, being scientific meant concern for only final causes and thus they abstracted society from their system and grounded it in nature and natural forces. Modern general equilibrium theorists have gone one step beyond the marginalists by abstracting from nature as well as from society. Only by leaving both social and natural factors out of their system have they been able to demonstrate the Invisible Hand theorem.[20] It should be pointed out that the solution of the existence, stability and optimality of equilibrium can only be achieved by abstracting from money, expectations and production – in a word, from capitalism. As Ingrao and Israel (p. 102) note:

> all the formal developments of the theory which most clearly and explicitly preaches 'the ability of a competitive system to achieve an allocation of resources that is efficient in some sense' have failed to show how the system can achieve equilibrium except 'by decree', namely, by the direct imposition of a system of equilibrium prices compatible with the features of the economy in question, which can only be achieved in a centrally planned economy.

It is the great irony of modern economic theory that in order to demonstrate Adam Smith's Invisible Hand, which was designed to counter Hobbes's call for a strong central government, modern general equilibrium theorists must take recourse in a Leviathan.

Under the natural law outlook, social phenomena and natural phenomena are two aspects of one reality, a reality which is determined and regulated by the principle of design. Under the influence of this outlook economic theorists have continually emulated natural scientists in the hope that they too would achieve similar results. Smith followed Newton and thus hoped to find the natural laws by observation – the final causes could be discovered by careful study of efficient causes. The marginalists emulated the physicists of their day and built models, based on natural factors alone, which resembled physics.[21] Modern general equilibrium theorists, in their adoption of the axiomatic method, are employing the methods of their contemporaries in theoretical physics and mathematics. The essential and infrequently asked question is: are social phenomena essentially different from natural phenomena, and if so, how applicable are the methods and models of the natural sciences for the social sciences?[22]

Notes

1. The author would like to thank Gary Mongiovi, Warren Samuels, Philip Mirowski, Paul Wendt and Tim Alborn for the helpful suggestions and comments.
2. See O'Brien (1975) chapters 1 and 2; Bonar (1893) chapters 7–12; Schumpeter (1954); Veblen (1919), essays 1–7 and Clark (1989a; 1988; 1989b; 1990).
3. For more on the moral aspects of natural law theories, see Robert Brown's *The Nature of Social Laws*.
4. Implicit in the condemnation of unnatural actions is the idea of the principle of design, which plays such an important role in Smith's system, see Clark (1988).
5. The creation of economics as a scientific pursuit is discussed in 'The Philosophical Foundations of "Scientific Economics" and the Concept of Equilibrium' (Clark, 1989c).
6. For Smith's natural law outlook, particularly the influences on it, see Clark (1988; 1990).
7. See Clark, 'Adam Smith and Society as an Evolutionary Process' (1990) for an examination into this dichotomy in Smith.
8. See chapter eight of Hume's (1972) *An Enquiry Concerning Human Understanding*. In the *Wealth of Nations* Smith writes:

    The difference of natural talents in different men is, in reality, much less than we are aware of; and the very different genius which appears to distinguish men of different professions, when grown up to maturity, is not upon many occasions so much the cause, as the effect of the division of labour. The difference between a philosopher and a common street porter, for example, seems to arise not so much from nature, as from habit, custom, and education (Smith, 1976a, pp. 28–9).

9. Yet Smith's materialistic explanations frequently show the influence of Montesquieu and the concern for social conditions. Thus, although the search for philosophical explanations is based in human nature, as are the criteria of evaluating competing theories, all this takes place under the requirement of certain conditions in the social environment. 'When law has established order and security, and subsistence ceases to be precarious, the curiosity of mankind is increased' (Smith, 1979, p. 50).
10. This in turn, Smith suggests in TMS, might be based on the natural instinct of persuasion. 'The desire of being believed, the desire of persuading, of leading and directing other people, seems to be one of the strongest of all our natural desires. It is, perhaps, the instinct upon which is founded the faculty of speech, the characteristical faculty of human nature' (p. 336).
11. On Smith's early and rude state and his use of conjectural history, Veblen (1919, p. 121) has written:

    The whole narrative, from the putative origin down, is not only supposititious, but it is merely a schematic presentation of what should have been the course of past development, in order to lead up to that ideal economic situation which would satisfy Adam Smith's preconceptions.

12. Marshall is an exception to this general trend, for he at least recognized the limitations of the natural law outlook and the adoption of the physical sciences as the model for the social sciences. Yet, he does not allow this skepticism to interfere with his developing a system based on the natural sciences (see Mirowski, 1984). In fact, Marshall's celebrated call for organic reasoning in economics is based on the belief that organic reasoning was just a more advanced form of mechanical reasoning, a commonly held view in Marshall's day.

13. In an early article Walras (1860) argued at length that economic science is based on natural forces.

14. See Clark (1989b) for a detailed analysis of the natural law elements in the marginal utility revolution.

15. Particularly forceful on this point is Menger, whose *Investigations* is largely concerned with arguing this point.

16. This is partially done in Clark (1989c; 1989a) and to a lesser extent in Clark (1987–8).

17. See Schumpeter (1954, p. 969) for the neo-classical argument on why the determination of a unique equilibrium is necessary for economics to be an 'exact science'.

18. Not only is it a narrowing of the boundaries, but as John B. Davis has shown, the adoption of the axiomatic method 'fails to provide an adequate analysis of reference, so that theories in the sciences which embody this approach cannot be said to be referentially adequate in the sense of anchoring their key concepts and expressions in reality' (1989, p. 425).

19. It is important to point out that the assumptions of modern general equilibrium theory are basically those of the marginalists, particularly with regard to human nature. On the usefulness of general equilibrium theory and its unrealistic assumptions, the single best critique is Kaldor (1972).

20. Actually they have yet to solve all three of their concerns about equilibrium, the problem of stability has yet to have been adequately resolved, and according to Ingrao and Israel will never be solved (Ingrao and Israel, 1985, p. 120).

21. This has been persuasively argued by Philip Mirowski (1984) who also notes that the marginalists did not fully comprehend the physics they were emulating and thus did not see the incompatibility of the two sciences.

22. This issue is partially discussed in Clark (1989a).

References

Becker, J. F. (1961), 'Adam Smith's theory of social science', *Southern Economic Journal*, **28**, July, pp. 13–21.

Blanche, R. (1962), *Axiomatics*, New York: Free Press.

Bonar, J. (1893), *Philosophy and Political Economy*, London: Swan Sorrenschein & Co.

Brown, R. (1984), *The Nature of Social Laws*, Cambridge: Cambridge University Press.

Clark, C. M. A. (1987–88), 'Equilibrium, market process and historical time', *Journal of Post Keynesian Economics*, **10**, (Winter), pp. 270–81.

Clark, C. M. A. (1988), 'Natural law influences on Adam Smith', *Quaderni di Storia dell Economia Politica*, **6**, pp. 59–83.

Clark, C. M. A. (1989a), 'Equilibrium for what?: Reflections on social order in economics', *Journal of Economic Issues*, **23**, June, pp. 597–606.

Clark, C. M. A. (1989b), 'The natural law preconceptions of Jevons, Menger and Walras', (unpublished).

Clark, C. M. A. (1989c), 'The philosophical foundations of "scientific economics" and the concept of equilibrium', paper delivered at the Eastern Economic Association meetings, Baltimore, Md., March 3.

Clark, C. M. A. (1990), 'Adam Smith and society as an evolutionary process', *Journal of Economic Issues*, **24**, (September), pp. 825–44.

Davis, J. B. (1989), 'Axiomatic general equilibrium theory and referentiality', *Journal of Post Keynesian Economics*, **11**, pp. 424–38.

Debreu, G. (1959), *The Theory of Value: An Axiomatic Analysis of Economic Equilibrium*, New Haven: Yale University Press.

Hahn, F. H. (1981), 'General equilibrium theory,' in Bell and Kristol, eds. *The Crisis in Economic Theory,* New York: Basic Books.

Hahn, F. H. (1982), 'On the notion of equilibrium in economics,' in *Macroeconomics and Equilibrium,* Cambridge: Cambridge University Press, [First published 1972].

Hobbes, T. (1964), *Leviathan,* New York: Washington Square Press. [First published 1651].

Hume, D. (1972), *Enquiries Concerning the Human Understanding and Concerning the Principles of Morals,* ed. L. A. Selby-Bigge, Oxford: Oxford University Press. [First published 1748;1751].

Ingrao, B. and Israel, G. (1985), 'General economic Equilibrium theory. A history of ineffectual paradigmatic shifts', *Fundamenta Scientiae,* **6,** pp. 1–45; 89–125.

Jevons, W.S. (1879), *The Theory of Political Economy,* 2nd ed. London: Macmillian. [First published 1871].

Kaldor, N. (1972), 'The irrelevance of equilibrium economics,' *The Economic Journal,* (Dec.), pp. 1237–49.

Menger, C. (1981), *Principles of Economics,* New York: New York University Press. [First published 1871].

Menger, C. (1985), *Investigations into the Method of the Social Sciences,* New York: New York University Press, [First published 1883].

Mini, P. (1974), *Philosophy and Economics,* Gainesville: University Press of Florida.

Mirowski, P. (1984), 'Physics and the "marginalist" revolution', *Cambridge Journal of Economics,* **8,** pp. 361–79.

Mirowski, P. (1989), *Against Mechanism: Protecting Economics From Science,* Totowa, New Jersey: Rowman & Littlefield.

Myers, M. L. (1983), *The Soul of Modern Economic Man,* Chicago: Chicago University Press.

O'Brien, D. P. (1975), *The Classical Economists,* Oxford: Oxford University Press.

Schumpeter, J. (1954), *History of Economic Analysis,* New York: Oxford University Press.

Smith, A. (1976a), *The Theory of Moral Sentiments,* ed. D. D. Raphael and A. L. Macfie, Oxford: Clarendon Press. [First published 1759].

Smith, A. (1976b), *An Inquiry into the Nature and Causes of the Wealth of Nations,* eds. R. H. Campbell and A. S. Skinner, Oxford: Clarendon Press. [First published 1776].

Smith, A. (1978), *Lectures on Jurisprudence,* eds. R. L. Meek, D. D. Raphael and P. G. Stein, Oxford: Clarendon Press.

Smith, A. (1979), *Essays on Philosophical Subjects,* edited by D. D. Raphael and A. S. Skinner, Oxford: Clarendon Press.[First published 1795].

Smith, A. (1983), *Lectures on Rhetoric and Belle Letters,* ed. J. C. Bryce, Oxford: Clarendon Press. [First published 1963].

Spengler, J. J. (1960), 'The problem of order in economic affairs' in Spengler and Allen (eds.), *Essays in Economic Thought,* Chicago: Rand and McNally & Company.

Veblen, T. (1898), 'Why is economics not an evolutionary science?' *Quarterly Journal of Economics,* **12,** (July). Reprinted in Veblen (1919).

Veblen, T. (1899–90), 'The preconceptions of economic science', *Quarterly Journal of Economics.* **13–14** Reprinted in Veblen (1919).

Veblen, T. (1909), 'The limitations of marginal utility', *Journal of Political Economy,* (17 Nov.). Reprinted in Veblen (1919).

Veblen, T. (1919), *The Place of Science in Modern Civilization and Other Essays,* New York: Huebsch.

Walras, L. (1860), 'Philosophie des Sciences Economiques', *Journal Des Economistes, Revue de la Science Economique et de la Statistique* 2d series, **25,** (2), February 15, pp. 196–206.

Walras, L. (1954), *Elements of Pure Economics,* translated by William Jaffe. Homewood, Ill: Irwin. [First published 1874–7].

Weintraub, E. R. (1985), *General Equilibrium Analysis,* Cambridge: Cambridge University Press.

Winch, D. (1972), 'Marginalism and the boundaries of economic science', in Black, Coats and Goodwin, (eds), *The Marginal Revolution in Economics,* Durham: Duke University Press, pp. 59–77.

Name Index

Abrahams, Lionel, 30, 33
Akerman, G., 119
Angell, Norman, *The Great Illusion*, 44

Bailey, Thomas, A., 56, 64, 65, 66
Barber, W.J., 57
Barker, D.A., 31
Barro, Robert, 105
Becker, James, 138
Bentham, Jeremy, 141
Blackett, Basil, 51
Böhm-Bawerk, E. von, 85, 88, 99, 119
Bonar Law, Andrew, 46
Borah, E., 55
Borah, W.E., 65
Bradbury, Lord, 70
Brailsford, H.N., 41
Brand, R.H.L., 47
Brems, H., 119
Brunner, Karl, 109
Burke, Edmund, 4, 8–10
Burmeister, E., 122, 123

Cagan, P., 106
Cannan, Edwin, 113
Cassel, Sir Ernest, 51
Cecil, Lord Robert, 47
Chalmers, Sir Robert, 33
Chamberlain, Austen, 33, 46–7, 50
Chandavarkar, A.G., 29, 32, 34
Chaudhuri, P., 29
Clark, C.M.A., 135, 137, 141
Clarke, P., 19–20
Clemenceau, Georges, 56, 65, 69
Clower, Robert, 105, 106, 108
Colander, D.C., 114
Craveth, Paul, 60
Crowe, E.A., 48
Cumberland, Richard, 137
Cunliffe, Lord, 49
Curzon, Lord, 46, 48

Davis, Norman, 68
Day, Clive, 57

Debreu, G., 142
di Modica, Giovanni, 72
di Viti de Marco, Antonio, 70, 72
Dobell, A.R., 122, 123
Drummond Fraser, Mrs V.R., 42
Dulles, John Foster, 56

Einaudi, Luigi, 72

Ferguson, C.E., 127
Fisher, Warren, 45
Foxwell, H.S., 29
Frankfurter, Felix, 55
Freeden, M., 3, 19, 20
Freud, Sigmund, 15
Friedman, Milton, 109
Frisch, Ragnar, 93

Galbraith, J.K., 15
Gesell, 21
Glazier, Mrs Evelyn Marr, 105
Graham, F.D., 97
Green, T.H., 20
Grilli, C., 73
Grossman, Herschel, 105, 111

Hahn, F.H., 143
Harcourt, G.C., 128
Harrod, R.F., 55, 65
Hawtrey, R.G., 41, 91, 92–3
Hayek, F.A., 102, 112
 see also subject index
Headlam-Morley, James, 47–8, 50
Helburn, S.W., 3
Hicks, John, 91
Hobbes, Thomas, *Leviathan*, 136–7, 143
Hobhouse, L.T., 20
Hobson, J.A., 20, 82
Hooks, D.L., 127
Hughes, William, 49
Hume, David, 109
Hunt, E.R., 15
Hutt, William, *see subject index*

147

Subject Index